CRICKET
On This Day

CRICKET
On This Day

*History, Facts & Figures
from Every Day of the Year*

PAUL DONNELLEY

FOREWORD BY DICKIE BIRD MBE

CRICKET
On This Day

History, Facts & Figures
from Every Day of the Year

All statistics, facts and figures are correct as of 1st August 2009.

© Paul Donnelley

Paul Donnelley has asserted his rights in accordance with the Copyright, Designs and Patents Act 1988 to be identified as the author of this work.

Published By:
Pitch Publishing Ltd,
A2 Yeoman Gate,
Durrington BN13 3QZ

Email: info@pitchpublishing.co.uk
Web: www.pitchpublishing.co.uk

First published 2009

A catalogue record for this book is available from the British Library.

10-digit ISBN: 1-9054116-0-X
13-digit ISBN: 978-1-9054116-0-3

Printed and bound in Malta by Gutenberg Press

Pour ma belle femme Karima…
bien sûr

FOREWORD

During my cricketing career I have read many, many books about the sport. A lot of the facts and comments in these books tend to repeat themselves. It is refreshing to find a book that gives readers some of the little known facts, with an interesting twist that I am sure many quiz experts will fall upon and use.

We can all relate to many interesting facts on cricket, games, players, grounds and things we have seen that are both serious and comical.

I am sure you will find the book of interest to you and in some cases it will bring certain incidents to mind. Indeed I have chronicled many in my own six books. This book takes it to a bigger field, to record incidents worldwide. Compiled in a diary form it makes easy reading, and offers facts and events that some have long forgotten or are reading about for the first time. This can be read in short bursts between overs, between innings, or as a travel companion for those long journeys between grounds.

It is a book you will return to again and again to recall certain incidents and confirm just when they actually happened. It is in a sense a reference book, without the formality of a reference book.

A delightful read, I hope you enjoy this informative, interesting book and the little known facts it reveals.

Dickie Bird, August 2009

ACKNOWLEDGEMENTS

Jeremy Beadle MBE que tu dormes en paix; Dickie Bird MBE, Rory Bremner, Paul Camillin, Coralie Eichholtz, Gavin Fuller, Les Smith, Mitchell Symons, and for their help on a day question Russell Ash, Rodney Castleden, Rodney Dale and Ian Harrison.

ABBREVIATIONS

BCCI .... Board of Control for Cricket in India
ECB .... England and Wales Cricket Board
ICC .... International Cricket Council
JPL .... John Player League
MCC .... Marylebone Cricket Club
ODI ....One Day International
PCA .... Professional Cricketers' Association
SAB .... South African Breweries
TCCB .... Test and County Cricket Board
WSC ....World Series Cricket

NICKNAMES

Aussies ....Australia
Kiwis .... New Zealand
Springboks .... South Africa
Windies .... West Indies

NOTE: Where known, the date of the event is the actual date of occurrence and not the date of the start of the match. For example, if you look up Malcolm Marshall in most reference books you will see that he made his Test debut against India on 15 December 1978. However, the anecdote about his dismissal and tears on the way back to the pavilion occurred on the second day of play – 16 December – and it is under this date that the story is recorded.

INTRODUCTION

Cricket is most popular in those parts of the world where the English have had the most influence which probably explains why it has never really taken off in Scotland or the United States of America. Yet cricket at various levels is played around the world in countries such as Denmark and Japan where you would least expect the last game of the gentleman to proliferate. One only has to consult that yellow-jacketed bible of the sport *Wisden Cricketers' Almanack* each April to read accounts of the sport internationally.

Cricket encompasses every aspect of the human condition. In this book you will read tales of sporting excellence, bravery, jealousy and derring do on and off the square. Cricketers have fought and died in the battlefields of the First and Second World Wars as well as losing their lives in 9/11 and the Bali bombs – a gentleman in white flannels is even a prime suspect in the Jack the Ripper murders. Cricketers have been murdered on golf courses and in the homes of madwomen. They have come under terrorist attack on the way to a Test ground. They have committed suicide because of financial and mental problems. In fact there is virtually no area of the human condition that a cricketer has not participated in. This small book is not intended to be a history of cricket but it will hopefully find favour with cricket fans young and old as they dip into stories about cricketers past and present. The book can be read in one sitting or dipped into at will or even used as a quiz book during the lunch or tea intervals or those interminable times in English summers when bad light or rain stops play.

Paul Donnelley, August 2009
www.pauldonnelley.com

CRICKET
On This Day

JANUARY

FRIDAY 1 JANUARY 1965

South Africa's captain Trevor Goddard won the toss and decided to bat in the third Test of the 1964-1965 series against England. The Springboks made 501 for 7 declared with opener Eddie Barlow making 138 and number three batsman Tony Pithey 154. England made 442 with 121 from captain Mike Smith. In their second innings South Africa made 346 while England were 15 for 0 at the close of play in the match, which ended in a draw. The game is remarkable in that twenty players took turns at bowling – all but wicketkeeper Jim Parks on the England side and his opposite number Denis Lindsay for the Springboks. It also marked the match when opening batsman Geoff Boycott returned his best bowling figures of 3 for 47 including two victims clean bowled. His opening partner in the second innings Ken Barrington also had his best bowling figures in a Test; three wickets for just four runs off 3.1 overs.

SATURDAY 1 JANUARY 1966

Doctor Who interrupted a Test match between England and Australia in "Volcano", the eighth episode of the adventure The Daleks' Master Plan. The commentary by Trevor (Roger Brierley) and Scott (Bruce Wightman) was disrupted when the Tardis landed on the pitch with England needing 78 runs in forty-five minutes to win.

THURSDAY 2 JANUARY 1879

Lord Harris became the first peer to captain an England Test side when he led his country to a 10-wicket defeat in the third ever contest between England and Australia. Harris won the toss and elected to bat but England tumbled to 26 for 7 at one stage before Harris and Charlie Absolom hit 85 between them to take the score to 113 all out. Fred Spofforth achieved the first Test hat-trick dismissing Vernon Royle, Francis McKinnon, 35th MacKinnon of MacKinnon, and Tom Emmett. Harris top scored in England's second innings but it was not enough and Australia needed just 19 to win – a target achieved in just three overs without loss.

TUESDAY 2 JANUARY 1894

Alexander Downes became the only bowler to take four wickets with consecutive balls in New Zealand first class cricket when playing for Otago against Auckland. He dismissed captain Rowland Holle, William Stemson, John Lundon and Henry Lawson.

TUESDAY 3 JANUARY 1882

Australia Jack Blackham became the first wicketkeeper to stump both openers in the same innings in a Test match when he claimed the scalps of England's Dick Barlow and George Ulyett in the first Test, held at Melbourne Cricket Ground. The feat would not be repeated in Australia until 1998-1999 when Ian Healy dismissed Mark Butcher and Alec Stewart.

THURSDAY 3 JANUARY 1929

Donald Bradman scored his maiden Test century at 5.30pm in his fourth Test innings. He had been batting for 226 minutes on the fifth day of the third Ashes Test at Melbourne. It was the first of his 29 Test hundreds, 19 of which were scored against England.

THURSDAY 4 JANUARY 1906

South Africa won a Test for the first time – they beat England at Old Wanderers, Johannesburg by one wicket in the first of five Tests. England won the toss and decided to bat. They made 184 and Jack Crawford scored the most runs with 44. England looked to be in pole position to win the match when they dismissed the Springboks for just 91 with only three South Africans making double figures and Walter Lees taking 5 for 34. England made 190 in their second innings with 51 coming from captain Plum Warner. Set a target of 284 South Africa were 134 for 6 at one stage. Their victory was thanks to a fine 81 from Gordon White who stayed at the crease for 265 balls over 250 minutes. (White was to die of his wounds on 17 October 1918 at Gaza, Palestine, aged 36.) It was finally Dave Nourse with an unbeaten 93 who led the South Africans to 287 for 9 and that narrowest of victories.

SATURDAY 5 JANUARY 1957

South Africa's Russell Endean became the first batsman in Test cricket to be given out handled the ball. The incident occurred at Newlands, Cape Town on the morning of the final day of the second Test. South Africa had begun the day on 41 for 2 with Endean not out on three. He was unable to add to his overnight tally when he was out in the most unusual fashion trying to fend off a delivery from Jim Laker (see 18 August 1951).

TUESDAY 5 JANUARY 1971

Australia and England contested the first limited overs international match when they met at Melbourne Cricket Ground. The match was played on what should have been the last day of the abandoned third Test and was billed as Australians v MCC. Each side was allowed to bowl 40 eight ball overs but in the end neither side needed their full allocation. MCC scored 190 all out off 39.4 overs while the Australians scored 191 for 5 off 34.6 overs. John Edrich, who opened the batting for England and scored 82, was the first Man of the Match.

WEDNESDAY 6 JANUARY 1982

Geoff Boycott left the Test cricket arena for the 108th and last time. In an international career that had started on 4 June 1964 and lasted 17 years, seven months and two days Boycott hit twenty centuries and forty-two half centuries among 8,114 runs over 193 innings with a top score of 246 not out and an average of 47.72. In his last match, played at Eden Gardens, Calcutta, opening the batting with Graham Gooch he scored a disappointing 18 and 6.

FRIDAY 6 JANUARY 1984

Australian wicketkeeping legend Rodney Marsh hung up his gloves for the last time after taking 343 catches and eleven stumpings in 96 Tests (the legend "caught Marsh bowled Lillee" was recorded an incredible 95 times in Test scorecards). The moustachioed Marsh would have undoubtedly played a hundred or more Tests for his country had he not signed for Kerry Packer's World Series Cricket circus. Remarkably, for such a devoted servant to Australia from May 2003 until June 2005 Marsh was an England selector. On his appointment he said, "If I'm still a selector when England next play Australia [in 2005] then I'll be rooting for England to win."

SATURDAY 7 JANUARY 1956

India's Vinoo Mankad and Pankaj Roy completed the world record opening partnership in Test cricket when they scored 413 against New Zealand in the first Madras Test to be held at the Corporation Stadium. They took 472 minutes to complete their task and became the first Indian batsmen to bat throughout an entire day of a Test match. Mankad was finally out for 231 while his partner scored 173. India declared on 537 for 3 and bowled out the Kiwis for 209 and 219 to win the match by an innings and 109 runs.

SUNDAY 8 JANUARY 1804

Cricket mentioned in print in Australia for the first time. *The Sydney Gazette* and *New South Wales Advertiser* reported: "The late intense weather has been very favourable to the amateurs of cricket who scarce have a day for the past month."

MONDAY 8 JANUARY 1962

Two days before the fifth and final Test between India and England the Indian selectors announced that Kripal Singh and Subhash Gupte had been dropped and E.A.S. Prasanna had been added. No official reason was given. Indian captain Nari Contractor said that they had been dropped for disciplinary reasons following the third Test in Delhi. The Indian side had stayed at the Imperial Hotel and the receptionist had accused the two players of chatting her up and inviting her to their room. Both players vigorously denied the allegation and the married Gupte said that Kripal had only asked for drinks to be brought to the room. At the hearing Gupte was ticked off by a selector for not doing more to stop his roommate from using the phone to which he replied, "He is a big man. How can I stop him?" Both players were dropped from the forthcoming tour of the West Indies and 32-year-old spinner Gupte never played for India again. Kripal was not selected for three years and then played just three Tests before being dropped for good. The Nawab of Pataudi commented, "What a shame India should lose two such good players over what was… a rather trivial incident quite unconnected with cricket."

MONDAY 9 JANUARY 2006

Australia (209 for 3) beat South Africa (114 all out) in the first international Twenty20 game to be held in Australia before a crowd of 38,894 people at Brisbane Cricket Ground, Woolloongabba, Brisbane. Oddly, rather than their names the players' shirts bore their nicknames.

FRIDAY 10 JANUARY 1930

New Zealand played their very first Test match – their opponents were England. It was an odd winter as simultaneously another England team was playing Test cricket against West Indies in the first rubber to be held in the Caribbean (see 11 January 1930). At Lancaster Park, Christchurch England fielded six debutants and one of them, Maurice Allom, in his eighth over took four wickets in five balls including a hat-trick. At one stage New Zealand were 21 for 7 but they rallied to make 112. It was a low-scoring Test but England won by eight wickets.

THURSDAY 10 JANUARY 1985

Bombay batsman Ravi Shastri emulated Gary Sobers' feat of hitting six sixes off a single over when he smashed Baroda's slow bowler Tilak Raj all over the Wankhede Stadium, Bombay on his way to 200 not out. Shastri reached his double century in 123 balls and took just 1 hour and 53 minutes.

SATURDAY 11 JANUARY 1930

England played their first Test in the Caribbean at Bridgetown's Kensington Oval, Barbados. The match ended in a draw. The Windies had six debutants and England two including Bill Voce. The West Indies side featured Ben Sealey, then the youngest Test cricketer at 17 years, 122 days, and still the youngest to play for the Windies, while England recalled George Gunn at the age of 50 – his last appearance in a Test had been before Sealey was born.

SUNDAY 11 JANUARY 1959

Pakistan opening batsman Hanif Mohammad scored a then first class world record of 499 while batting for Karachi against Bahawalpur in the Quaid-e-Azam Trophy semi final at Karachi Parsi Institute Ground. Karachi won the toss and elected to field. Bahawalpur were all out for 185 and Karachi made 772 for 7 declared with Wallis Mathias also hitting a century. Bahawalpur were dismissed in their second innings for 108 which meant that Karachi won by an innings and 479 runs. In his autobiography, *Playing For Pakistan*, Mohammad wrote, "Nearing my triple-century, I was wearing out. I told [my captain and brother, Wazir Mohammad] it was a bit too much, but he said no, keep playing." That night Wazir had his brother massaged with olive oil to ensure he was relaxed. "There were two deliveries left in the day's play, and I noticed the scoreboard showing me on 496," he recalled and he became worried that his brother might declare so he took off for a reckless single. When the fielder did not take the ball cleanly, Mohammad returned for a second – the throw beat him by a yard and a half. He had thought that he was on 497 and did not find the actual score was 499 until he looked up at the scoreboard as he traipsed off. He was furious with himself. "Had I known I was batting on 498, I would have waited for the last delivery to get the required runs. After I got out, the Bahawalpur captain [Mohammad Ramzan] came to the dressing room with his team to congratulate me. He said, 'See, I told you we'd get you out at some point. And at least we didn't let you make 500'." Hanif Mohammad received congratulatory telegrams from around the world but the one that pleased him most came from Don Bradman.

TUESDAY 12 JANUARY 1864

Lancashire CCC founded by the leading members of the Manchester Cricket Club. Lancashire first won the County Championship in 1897.

WEDNESDAY 12 JANUARY 2005

The first Twenty20 game to be played in Australia was held at the Western Australia Cricket Association Ground in Perth between the Western Warriors and the Victorian Bushrangers before a crowd of 20,700.

FRIDAY 13 JANUARY 1933

The third Test of the Bodyline series began in Adelaide. England (341 and 412) beat Australia (222 and 193) by 338 runs. Australian captain Bill Woodfull commented, "There are two sides out there. One is trying to play cricket, the other is not. The game is too good to be spoilt."

TUESDAY 13 JANUARY 1981

The narrowest of victories as New Zealand beat Australia by just one run in the Benson and Hedges World Series Cup at Sydney Cricket Ground. New Zealand won the toss and decided to bat and made 220 for 8 from their fifty overs. Opener John Wright hit a 78, which won him the man of the match award. In response Australia made 219 for 7 with Doug Walters unbeaten on 50, Rod Marsh on 49 and Trevor Chappell and Shaun Graf both run out.

SATURDAY 14 JANUARY 1978

The first "Supertest" between WSC Australia and WSC World XI began at R.A.S. Showground, Sydney. WSC Australia batted first and scored 304 off 82.7 eight ball overs. Bruce Laird scored 106 but the next highest scorer was captain Ian Chappell way behind on 44. Springbok Mike Proctor who was unable to play Test cricket because of apartheid took 4 for 33 and West Indian Joel Garner returned figures of 3 for 71. In their first innings WSC World XI hit 290 with a century from Viv Richards and 57 from Barry Richards, another South African denied international cricket. Max Walker took 7 for 88 and Gary Gilmour picked up the other three wickets at a cost of 103. WSC Australia collapsed in the second innings and were all out for 128 with Martin Kent, one of the few non-international players signed by Kerry Packer, scoring 31. WSC World XI needed 143 to win and achieved the target with the loss of six wickets. The match, originally intended to last for five days, was extended to six to ensure a result.

FRIDAY 15 JANUARY 1904

Australian left-hander Clem Hill became the first batsman to score 2,000 runs in Test cricket and achieved the feat on his home ground, the Adelaide Oval, and against England. He was also the first player to score 3,000 runs in Test cricket and achieved the feat on the same ground in January 1911.

SATURDAY 15 JANUARY 1977

England fast bowler John Lever accused of cheating in the third Test against India at M.A. Chidambaram Stadium, Chepauk, Madras. England had won the toss, decided to bat and made 262. Lever and fellow pace man Bob Willis wore gauze strips stuck above their eyebrows by Vaseline to stop the sweat running into their eyes but both quickly discarded them, Willis straightaway and Lever after one over but some complained that Lever was using the Vaseline to shine the ball, in contravention of Law 46. The Indian authorities confiscated the ball and sent the strips to be analysed. That did not settle the matter and they asked MCC to deal with it and they absolved both men of any misdemeanour. And England won by 200 runs.

MONDAY 16 JANUARY 1598

John Derrick, a 59-year-old coroner, was involved in a legal dispute over an area of land in Guildford, Surrey. Derrick stated that "when I was a scholler in the free school of Guldeford, I and several of my fellowes did runne and play there are krickett and other plaises". Therefore, it can be ascertained that cricket was played at Guildford in the 1550s during the reign of Queen Mary I.

MONDAY 16 JANUARY 1933

During the third Test of the Bodyline series at Adelaide a demon delivery by Harold Larwood hit Bert Oldfield on the head and the 32,000 crowd went wild. Mounted police stood in readiness outside the ground in case there was a pitch invasion and inside the ground police took position around the boundary rope. However, nothing more serious occurred than fruit being thrown at Douglas Jardine.

SATURDAY 17 JANUARY 1925

The man who played Test cricket for two countries and became the father of Pakistani cricket, Abdul Hafeez Kardar, was born at Lahore in the Punjab. A left-handed batsman, he made his Test debut for India against England at Lord's on 22 June 1946 and was known as Abdul Hafeez until 1947. He made 43 as the Indians led by the Nawab of Pataudi Senior were bowled out for 200 with Alec Bedser taking 7 for 49. Despite poor performances from Len Hutton (7) and Denis Compton (0) England made 428 thanks to a double century from Joe Hardstaff (205 not out). In their second innings India were bowled out for 275 with Alec Bedser taking 4 for 96 to bring his tally for the match to 11 for 145. One of his victims for a duck was Hafeez. Len Hutton and Cyril Washbrook easily made the runs England needed for a 10-wicket victory. After the summer tour, he stayed in England and went to Oxford to read Philosophy, Politics and Economics. He signed to play county cricket for Warwickshire and married the club chairman's daughter. When Pakistan played their first Test match in 1952 the now Abdul Hafeez Kardar was team captain, a position he held for 23 matches. He led the team to victory against all the then Test-playing nations apart from South Africa, whom they never met. On his retirement he became chairman of selectors, and president of Pakistan's Board of Control from 1972 to 1977. He was short-tempered and took any hint of criticism as a personal affront. He resigned in protest against government interference. He died aged 71 on 21 April 1996.

SATURDAY 17 JANUARY 1931

On the second day of the third Test against Australia in Brisbane, George Headley hit an unbeaten 102 to become the only player under 21 to score four Test centuries. Headley was born on 30 May 1909 at Colon, Panama where his father was helping to build the canal. Aged ten he was taken to Jamaica and prepared to study dentistry in America, but while waiting for a passport played against a touring English side scoring 78 in the first match and 211 in the second. He made his Test debut for West Indies on 11 January 1930.

WEDNESDAY 18 JANUARY 1933

Bodyline bowling threatened the political peace between England and Australia in an oddly worded telegram sent to MCC. During the third Test at Adelaide fast bowler Harold Larwood had developed bodyline bowling into such an art that Aussie batsmen lived in fear of injury. After three were seriously hit and the irate fans clamoured for revenge, the Australian Cricket Board of Control telegraphed MCC in London, "In our opinion, it is unsportsmanlike. Unless it is stopped at once it is likely to upset the friendly relations between Australia and England." Ironically, Larwood emigrated to Australia where he was treated as a folk hero although one small child was heard to say, "He doesn't look like a murderer."

TUESDAY 18 JANUARY 2000

When England toured South Africa in 1999-2000 they lost two of the first four Test matches giving the rubber to the Springboks. On the first day of play (14 January 2000) of the fifth and final Test at Supersport Park, Centurion, South Africa scored 155 for 6 before rain prevented play on the next three days. South African captain Hansie Cronje proposed to England captain Nasser Hussain that his team bat until they reached 250 at which time they would declare, and both sides would forfeit an innings leaving England 251 to win. Hussain agreed and in the end the Springboks made 248 for 8 declared (Cronje was out for a duck). At the time the laws allowed only one side to forfeit an innings so England were recorded as 0 for 0 declared. England eventually made 251 for 8 and won by two wickets. It was later revealed that Cronje had been asked by a bookie to ensure the match did not end without a positive result.

WEDNESDAY 19 JANUARY 1977

England beat India by 200 runs at Madras Cricket Club Ground, Chepauk, Madras in the third Test to win the first series in India for 43 years. Bob Willis, John Lever and Derek Underwood picked up the second innings wickets as India collapsed to 83 all out.

MONDAY 19 JANUARY 2004

Former Australian Test cricketer David Hookes died in the evening aged 48 after being punched by hotel bouncer Zdravko Micevic, a former boxer, outside the Beaconsfield Hotel in St Kilda, Melbourne where Hookes had been drinking with Victoria and South Australia players following the former's victory in a match the previous day. Hookes had fallen and hit his head, and had a heart attack caused by shock. He was taken to Alfred Hospital, Prahran, Melbourne and put on a life support machine. He died not long after being taken off the machine. On 22 August 2005 Micevic, 23, went on trial for Hookes's manslaughter. He was acquitted on 12 September 2005 after the jury deliberated for five days. Of his career, Hookes said, "I suspect history will judge me harshly as a batsman because of my modest record in 23 Tests and I can't complain about that."

MONDAY 20 JANUARY 1958

Hanif Mohammad went out to bat for Pakistan in their second innings against West Indies at Bridgetown, Barbados – their first Test against West Indies. Little could the Windies or the spectators know that he would still be there four days later as he compiled the longest individual innings in all first class cricket occupying the crease for 16 hours and ten minutes to score 337 of a total of 626 for 6 declared. Remarkably, his innings did not include a single six and despite the hostile bowling his pads were thin and slender and his thigh pad was a rolled up hotel towel. A myth has grown up around the knock that the ball never hit Mohammad's pads. The man himself disputes this, "Well, almost. The pitch had some rough areas and a few times the ball did misbehave, which made me miss the line. This one delivery, I even thought I was lbw. But fate was with me. [Bowler Eric] Atkinson was the only one who really troubled me. He used to put a lot of cream in his hair. That may have had something to do with the fact that he managed to swing it both ways, and swing it late." The match ended in a draw thanks to Hanif Mohammad.

TUESDAY 20 JANUARY 2004

Mark Vermeulen hit on the head by Irfan Pathan during Zimbabwe's VB Series campaign in Australia. Afterwards his behaviour was erratic – in 2006 he was banned for ten years from playing cricket in England after threatening spectators during a Central Lancashire League match. The ban was reduced on appeal to three with the second and third suspended. In October of the same year he was arrested for arson at the offices of the Harare Sports Club and the National Academy. His defence counsel stated at his trial in January 2008 that he was suffering psychiatric problems including partial complex epilepsy and he was acquitted. However, he was a little eccentric even before the accident – in 1996 while playing for Prince Edward High School in Harare he walked off with the stumps after disagreeing with an lbw decision and locked himself in the dressing room. In 2003 he was sent home from the Zimbabwe tour of England when he refused to stop a ball at Hove because it was "too cold" and later would not board the team coach, preferring to make his own way.

WEDNESDAY 21 JANUARY 1948

George Headley became the first black player to captain West Indies, when he led the side against England in the first Test of the 1947-1948 rubber, at Kensington Oval, Bridgetown, Barbados.

MONDAY 21 JANUARY 1991

While on the Ashes tour of 1990-1991 David Gower and John Morris hired two 1938 Tiger Moth biplanes and decided to buzz the match between Queensland and an England XI at Cararra Oval. They had also intended to drop water bombs on their colleagues but were dissuaded from doing so by the pilots. Both players were fined £1,000 and the planes cost £27 to hire.

WEDNESDAY 22 JANUARY 1879

A thousand people gathered on a frozen dam near Brampton to watch Chesterfield play Sheffield in a game of cricket on ice. The game was played under the usual rules except a player had to retire when he had scored 25 runs. Chesterfield scored 113 in their knock with Test cricketer Harry Charlwood and C.H. Trown scoring the maximum 25 and Joe Rowbotham taking 4 wickets. Sheffield scored 125 for 7 with four players hitting 25 including Rowbotham.

THURSDAY 22 JANUARY 1970

South African Barry Richards made his debut in the first Test against Australia at Newlands, Cape Town, which the Springboks won by 170 runs. By the time his Test career ended (after just four matches because of South Africa's sporting isolation) he had averaged 72.57. Other Springbok debutants in the Test were middle-order batsman Lee Irvine, wicketkeeper Dennis Gamsy and left-arm spinner Grahame Chevalier.

SATURDAY 23 JANUARY 1993

While captaining the England XI against an Indian Under-25 XI at Cuttack in India Graham Gooch became the twenty-third player to score one hundred first-class centuries when he hit 102 before retiring hurt at tea when the score was on 218. Oddly, at the time Gooch did not know if he had scored a century of tons because the following week the ICC was to decide if his century on the rebel tour of South Africa in 1982 was a first class match. The ICC declared that the game was not first class but their decision was ignored by most statistical organisations.

GRAHAM GOOCH HIT A ONE HUNDREDTH HUNDRED IN JANUARY 1993

TUESDAY 23 JANUARY 2001

West Indian wicketkeeper Ridley Jacobs played a blinder against Zimbabwe in the 50-over Carlton Series at Sydney Cricket Ground and still ended up on the losing side. West Indies won the toss and decided to field. They took 177 minutes and 47.2 overs to bowl out Zimbabwe for 138. Jacobs took five catches and was in the process of taking a record-breaking sixth (Brian Murphy) when his cap fell off and hit the ball, thus incurring a five-run penalty. In the end the five runs were unimportant as Zimbabwe bowled the West Indians out for 91 to win by 47 runs. It could have been much worse for the Windies; at one stage they were 31 for 8.

TUESDAY 24 JANUARY 1950

Australia beat South Africa at Kingsmead, Durban in the third Test by five wickets as a tactical blunder let the Aussies off the hook. The Springboks made 311 in their first innings and then skittled Australia for 75. Hugh Tayfield took 7 for 23. Springbok skipper Dudley Nourse, 39, decided not to make Australia follow on and then saw his side bowled out for 99. Ian Johnson took 5 for 34 and Bill Johnston captured 4 wickets for 39. Australia needed 336 to win and made it with the loss of just five wickets thanks in no small measure to 151 not out from Neil Harvey.

SUNDAY 24 JANUARY 1999

West Indies beat South Africa by 43 runs in a one day international at Buffalo Park, East London. The Windies hit 292 for 9 in their fifty overs, which was the highest one-day total against South Africa in their homeland. Oddly, 258 of the runs came from just two players: Shivnarine Chanderpaul (150) and Carl Hooper (108). None of the rest of the team managed double figures apart from Extras who scored 13. There were three ducks and Shaun Pollock took 6 for 35. Hansie Cronje's South Africa were bowled out for 249.

FRIDAY 25 JANUARY 1935

England Test cricketer Vallance Jupp convicted at Northampton Assizes of manslaughter and sentenced to nine months in jail. He had been driving his car on the wrong side of the road when he hit a motorcyclist, killing the pillion passenger. Jupp was released in early June 1935 after serving four-and-a-half months but did not resume his cricket career until 1936. He died in 1960.

FRIDAY 25 JANUARY 1974

Christopher Dey became the only non-striker in first class cricket to be given out handled the ball. Playing for Northern Transvaal against Orange Free State in the SAB Currie Cup at Ramblers Cricket Club Ground, Bloemfontein, Dey had scored 20 when backing up he bumped into a fielder and fell over with the ball lodged under his body. While still lying on the ground the Orange Free State team appealed and the umpire gave him out.

TUESDAY 26 JANUARY 1993

West Indies beat Australia by one run at Adelaide Oval to achieve the narrowest ever Test victory. The Windies under the captaincy of Richie Richardson won the toss and elected to bat. Allan Border's Australia bowled them out for 252; Brian Lara was top scorer on 52 and Merv Hughes was the most successful Australian bowler taking 5 for 64. Australia made 213 and that man Hughes was top scorer with 43. Curtly Ambrose took 6 for 74. In their second innings West Indies only made 146, 72 of which came from captain Richardson. The Australians needed 186 to win but thanks to man of the match Ambrose and Courtney Walsh, they were all out for 184.

MONDAY 26 JANUARY 1998

In a South African first class match between Northerns and Gauteng at Johannesburg, Gauteng lost seven wickets when the score was on 12. It is believed to be the first time seven wickets have been lost on the same score since the MCC lost seven for 0 against Surrey in 1872. Incidentally, Gauteng were bowled out for 74 and lost the match by 236 runs.

WEDNESDAY 27 JANUARY 1864

The first first class match in New Zealand began at South Dunedin Recreation Ground between Otago and Canterbury. Canterbury won the toss and opted to field. Otago were all out for 78. Top scorer was James Fulton who hit 25. For Canterbury R. Taylor took six wickets for 21. Canterbury were all out for 34 but George Sale was the only batsman not to trouble the scorers. Otago made 74 in their second innings and then bowled Canterbury out for 42 with F. MacDonald taking 6 for 17. Otago won by 76 runs. Seventeen players made their first class debuts in the match but five of the Otago team had previously appeared in first-class matches for Victoria. Oddly, six-ball overs were used for the first innings and four-ball ones for the second.

SUNDAY 27 JANUARY 1985

England beat India in a one day international in Chandigarh by seven runs. It was the fifth of the series and England were already leading 3-1 when the heavens opened and the ground was flooded. Rather than abandoning the game, the authorities decided to reduce it to a 15-over slog. India won the toss and decided to field. In terrible conditions England made 121 for 6 from their allocated overs. After their fifteen overs India were on 114 for 5 and England wrapped up the Charminar Challenge Cup 4-1.

FRIDAY 28 JANUARY 1887

Australia's Percy McDonnell became the first Test captain to win a toss and ask the other side to bat. He won the call at the Sydney Cricket Ground in the first Test against England and it seemed his strategy paid off when he used just two bowlers (Charlie Turner 6 for 15 and J.J. Ferris 4 for 27) and England were dismissed for just 45 with only one player (George Lohmann) making double figures – 17. Australia then made 119 before England returned to the fray and hit 184 (Ferris taking 5 for 76 and just missing by one ten wickets in a match). England then bowled Australia out for 97 (Billy Barnes 6 for 28) to win the game by 13 runs.

THURSDAY 28 JANUARY 1960

The fifth Test ended between India and Australia at Eden Gardens, Calcutta in a draw. It was the first match in which a batsman – Motganhalli Jaisimha – batted on every day of the game.

FRIDAY 29 JANUARY 1993

The first Test of the 1993 series began between India and England at Eden Gardens, Calcutta. It marked the recall to the England side of former captain Mike Gatting after an almost four-year absence. He retained his place when the Australians toured in the summer of 1993 but the selectors' decision upset Geoff Boycott who commented, "If I were being polite, I'd say Gatt is a little long in the tooth, somewhat immobile and carried too much weight. But I prefer straight talking, so I'm saying what I really think. Gatt is too old, too slow and too fat."

THURSDAY 29 JANUARY 1998

The first Test between West Indies and England at Sabina Park, Kingston, Jamaica became the first Test to be abandoned because of a poor pitch and dangerous wicket. England won the toss and decided to bat but after 10.1 overs and 56 minutes they were 17 for 3 and the players had been hit seven times. The England physiotherapist Wayne Morton spent more time on the pitch than some of the batsmen. The umpires Steve Bucknor and Srinivasaraghavan Venkataraghavan stopped play and after ten minutes of discussion the players left the field. Ninety minutes later, the match was abandoned.

SATURDAY 30 JANUARY 1892

Bobby Abel became the first Englishman to carry his bat in a Test match when he was 132 not out in the first innings of the second Test against Australia played at Association Ground, Sydney. In the second innings he only made 1 and Australia won by 72 runs.

FRIDAY 30 JANUARY 2009

Cricket statistician Bill Frindall died aged 69 of legionnaires' disease. At the time of his death, he was the longest serving member of *Test Match Special*.

MONDAY 31 JANUARY 1927

Umpire Harry Bagshaw died at Crowden, near Glossop, aged 65. He was a competent but unflashy player for Derbyshire and Barnsley CC for whom he once scored 220 and took all ten wickets in an innings against Wakefield in 1891. He took his umpiring seriously and when he was interred he insisted on being buried in his umpire's coat and with a cricket ball in his hand. His gravestone bore broken stumps, dislodged bails and an umpire's hand signalling "Out".

WEDNESDAY 31 JANUARY 1979

Honourable wicketkeeper Bob Taylor walked on 97 during the fifth Ashes Test at Adelaide Oval. Facing fast bowler Rodney Hogg, Taylor gave the ball the merest leg-side tickle before wicketkeeper Kevin Wright scooped it up. Without waiting for the umpire to raise his arm, Taylor made his way back to the pavilion – it would have been his only Test century.

CRICKET
On This Day

FEBRUARY

MONDAY 1 FEBRUARY 1932

Australia's Don Bradman stranded on 299 not out in the fourth Test against South Africa, at Adelaide. With the score at 513 for 9, last man "Pud" Thurlow attempted the run that would have given The Don his triple century only to be run out. As some consolation, Australia won the match by 10 wickets.

SUNDAY 1 FEBRUARY 1981

The last under-arm delivery in a limited-over international was the last ball of the last over of a match between Australia and New Zealand – and it was considered so underhand that the practice was banned in Australia the following week. It was the third 50-over match of a best-of-five World Cup Series, Australia and New Zealand having won a game apiece. Australia batted first and made 235 for 4. New Zealand replied with 221 for 6 in 49 overs, leaving them with a target of fifteen runs from the final over to win. Trevor Chappell had the responsibility of not conceding those fifteen runs, and it must have been with some trepidation that he stepped up to bowl the final over. Richard Hadlee hit the first for four. Eleven required. Chappell bowled Hadlee with the second. Ian Smith hit the third and fourth for two each. Seven required. Chappell bowled Smith with the fifth. New Zealand batsman Brian McKechnie came in knowing that he must score six off the final ball to tie the game, which under World Series rules would have forced a replay. It was an unlikely scenario but Aussie captain Greg Chappell knew that McKechnie, an All Black as well as a cricketer, had the power to do it. So captain Greg instructed his younger brother to bowl the last ball under-arm, thus making it impossible for McKechnie to hit a six. After discussing the legality with the umpires (under-arm deliveries were already outlawed in English one-day games), Trevor did as Greg had ordered – to the disgust of the crowd, the batsman, the New Zealand Prime Minister, the Australian Cricket Board and most of the cricketing world. Even Greg Chappell later conceded that his decision was a mistake. The ball rolled along the wicket and all McKechnie could do was to block it – and then throw down his bat in protest. New Zealand PM Robert Muldoon described Chappell's decision as an act of cowardice appropriate to a team clad in yellow.

TUESDAY 2 FEBRUARY 1864

Middlesex CCC founded at the London Tavern, Bishopsgate. In 1903 Middlesex won the County Championship for the first time.

TUESDAY 2 FEBRUARY 1993

The ICC declared that the rebel tour to South Africa in 1982 was not first class and reduced Graham Gooch's centuries total to 99. Most statistical organisations ignored their decision. It also announced that the next World Cup would be held on the subcontinent in India, Pakistan and Sri Lanka despite a previous assurance that it would take place in England.

MONDAY 3 FEBRUARY 1851

The first peer to captain England George Robert Canning Harris, 4th Baron Harris, was born at St Ann's, Trinidad where his father was governor. He succeeded his father to the peerage in 1872 and made his first appearance as England captain on his Test debut in the third contest between the two countries. He won two of his four Tests as English captain, losing one and drawing the other. He was unbeaten on English soil when he led the team. On his retirement Harris went into politics and was Under-Secretary of State for India from 25 June 1885 until February 1886, then Parliamentary Under-Secretary of State for War from 4 August 1886 to 1890 in the Conservative Government. He served as Governor of the Presidency of Bombay in British India from 1890 to 1895 (see above).

SUNDAY 3 FEBRUARY 1974

England all-rounder Tony Greig ran out Alvin Kallicharran then on 142 not out as he and Bernard Julien headed off at close of play. West Indies were 274 for 6 in the first Test at the Queen's Park Oval in Port-of-Spain, Trinidad when Julien blocked the final ball of the day. Before umpire Douglas Sang Hue could call time the batsmen headed for the pavilion and Greig picked up the ball and broke Kallicharran's wicket. Since time had not been called, the umpire raised a finger. Once the players were off the pitch the crowd rioted and laid siege to the pavilion. To save the rubber and possibly Tony Greig's neck the England team withdrew the appeal and Kallicharran was reinstated, the only time this had happened in Test cricket. The next day Kallicharran took his score to 158. West Indies won the match by 7 wickets but the incident did nothing to help Greig's reputation.

MONDAY 4 FEBRUARY 1895

Bobby Peel of England became the first batsman to be stumped for nought in both innings of a Test on the same day as England collapsed to an Australian victory of an innings and 147 runs at Sydney Cricket Ground.

SUNDAY 4 FEBRUARY 1990

New Zealand pace man Richard Hadlee dismissed Sanjay Manjrekar to become the first bowler to take four hundred wickets in Test cricket. He achieved the feat on his home ground of Lancaster Park, Christchurch when he was 38 years old and it had taken him eighty Tests. Later that summer he was knighted in the Queen's Birthday Honours List.

THURSDAY 5 FEBRUARY 1970

Off-spinner John Traicos made his Test debut for South Africa against Australia at Kingsmead, Durban. He took three wickets in the game – the second Test – the Springboks' last series before international sporting exile. South Africa won by an innings and 129 runs. Traicos also played in the third and fourth Tests before his international career ended for 22 years and 222 days. In October 1992 he was the only member of the first Zimbabwe Test side who had previous experience – he took 5 for 86. Traicos who was born at Zagazig, Egypt with the unusual first name Athanasios fled Zimbabwe for political reasons in 1997 and moved to Perth, Western Australia.

THURSDAY 5 FEBRUARY 2009

Controversial Sri Lankan spinner Muttiah Muralitharan became the most successful bowler in One Day Internationals when he captured the wicket of Gautham Gambhir at Colombo – his 503rd wicket to overtake the previous record holder Wasim Akram of Pakistan.

TUESDAY 6 FEBRUARY 1872

Charles Alcock appointed secretary of Surrey CCC, a position he was to hold until the time of his death on 26 February 1907. In 1880 he was instrumental in organising the first Test match in England (see 6 September), and two years later founded the magazine *Cricket* that he edited until his death. He was also editor of *James Lillywhite's Cricketers' Annual* for twenty-nine years and for many years he arranged the fixtures for tourists to England. Oddly, he found himself captain of France in a cricket match against Germany. He was also heavily involved in football – he created the FA Cup and captained Wanderers, the first winners, and also led England against Scotland in 1875.

TUESDAY 6 FEBRUARY 1923

Victoria achieved the greatest winning margin in Australian cricket when they beat Tasmania by an innings and 666 runs at Melbourne Cricket Ground. Tasmania won the toss and decided to bat in the timeless match and made 217 all out, Colin Newton on an undefeated 49 the top scorer. Victoria then made 1,059 all out with captain Bill Ponsford making 429. Tasmanian bowler Ashley Facy had his career figures wrecked by returning 2 for 228. A dispirited Tasmanian side was then all out for 176. Oddly five players made their first class debuts for Tasmania and seven for Victoria during the match.

WEDNESDAY 7 FEBRUARY 1838

The first reference to sledging appeared in the *Commercial Journal*, which noted that it was the "low slang and insulting remarks so often resorted to by Australians".

THURSDAY 7 FEBRUARY 2008

Pakistani seam bowler Rahatullah disappeared as he journeyed to Arbab Niaz Stadium where he was due to join the North West Frontier Province squad. On 10 February his bullet-ridden body was discovered at Peshawar. Early reports stated that he had been decapitated. He was 18 years old. He had toured Australia and played against India with the Pakistan Under-19 team and represented Peshawar in three first-class matches in the 2007-2008 Quaid-i-Azam Trophy. His murder remains unsolved.

SATURDAY 8 FEBRUARY 1902

Toddles Dowson, a 5ft tall left-arm leg-break bowler began his account for R.A. Bennett's XI against Jamaica at Kingston and when he had finished on the 10 February he had taken 16 wickets for 58 (8 for 21 – career best – and 8 for 37), the best match figures in first class cricket in the West Indies.

WEDNESDAY 8 FEBRUARY 2006

Michael Vaughan awarded an honorary doctorate by Sheffield Hallam University although the recipient could not be present – he was in Pakistan with the England team.

TUESDAY 9 FEBRUARY 1904

MCC bowled out Victoria at Melbourne Cricket Ground for just 15 – the lowest first class total in Australia – and won by eight wickets. Victoria won the toss and elected to bat and in their first innings made a respectable 299 all out with Percy McAlister making 139 and Wilf Rhodes taking 6 for 62. MCC were then all out for 248. With one man absent hurt, Victoria came out to bat and were dismissed for 15 with Rhodes taking 5 for 6 and Ted Arnold 4 for 8. Only five Victoria players got off the mark and captain Harry Trott led the fight with 9. It took just 12.1 overs and forty-five minutes to dismiss the home side and MCC made their target losing two wickets in the process.

SUNDAY 9 FEBRUARY 1986

Mohinder Amarnath of India became the first batsman to be dismissed for handling the ball in One Day Internationals. He was on 15 at Melbourne Cricket Ground in the second match between Australia and India. Australia won by 7 wickets with sixteen balls remaining (see 22 October 1989).

FRIDAY 10 FEBRUARY 1888

The only Test of the 1887-1888 Ashes season began at Association Ground, Sydney. The England team was made up of two touring sides, one led by George F. Vernon and the other by Arthur Shrewsbury. A timeless Test, Australia won the toss and decided to field. Rain had done much to damage the pitch and England made 113 all out with Shrewsbury the top scorer with 44. Charlie Turner took 5 for 44. Australia were bowled out for 42 with only Tom Garrett making double figures (10). George Lohmann, who would be *Wisden* Cricketer of the Year in 1889, took 5 for 17 while Bobby Peel took a similar number of wickets and was just one run more expensive. England made 137 in their second innings with Turner taking a Test career best of 7 for 43 bringing his haul for the match to 12 for 87. England then skittled out Australia for 82 – the first time the Aussies had been bowled out for less than 100 twice in the same match – to win by 126 runs. Oddly, only seven bowlers were used in the match – four for the home side and three for the tourists.

SUNDAY 10 FEBRUARY 1952

India won their first Test match when they beat England by an innings and eight runs, at M.A. Chidambaram Stadium, Chepauk, Madras. It was their twenty-fifth attempt at trying to win a Test and they had made five changes from thee previous match, which they lost by eight wickets. The arrangements for the match were changed when the death of H.M. King George VI was announced on the afternoon of the first day and the rest day was moved to the second day. The hero of the match for India was Vinoo Mankad who took 8 for 55 in England's first innings, scored 22, and took 4 for 53 as India won the match within four days.

MONDAY 11 FEBRUARY 1907

Cricket commentator E.W. (Ernest William) "Jim" Swanton born at Forest Hill, London. He wrote for *The Daily Telegraph* between 1946 and 1975 and later commentated on *Test Match Special*. Not everyone was enamoured of Swanton. One colleague said, "Jim is such a snob that he won't travel in the same car as his chauffeur."

FRIDAY 11 FEBRUARY 1921

The fourth Test began between Australia and England at Melbourne Cricket Ground, the second of the rubber to be held at the MCG. England won the toss and decided to bat and were all out for 284 with Harry Makepeace making a career best 117. At one stage Australia were 153 for 5 when their 22-stone captain waddled to the wicket. Warwick Armstrong was suffering from malaria when he went to the crease but reportedly cleared his head by downing two large whiskies. Apocryphal or not, he made an unbeaten 123 and led his team to victory by eight wickets.

THURSDAY 12 FEBRUARY 1857

Yorkshire slow left-arm bowler Bobby Peel born at Churwell, Leeds. He played in 20 Tests and took 101 wickets. While playing for Yorkshire against Lancashire in a County Championship game in 1897 Peel was drunk and reportedly urinated on the pitch. His captain Lord Hawke sent him off the field and Peel later recalled, "Lord Hawke put his arm round me and helped me off the ground – and out of first class cricket. What a gentleman!"

FRIDAY 12 FEBRUARY 1965

Future umpire Ken Palmer played in his only Test when he represented a depleted-through-injury England side in the fifth Test against South Africa at St George's Park, Port Elizabeth. Batting at number eleven he made 10 in his only innings. With the ball he was less successful returning match figures of 1 for 189 – the second-worst in England's Test history.

THURSDAY 13 FEBRUARY 1896

C.B. Fry made his Test debut against South Africa at St George's Park, Port Elizabeth in the first Test of the 1895-1896 series. It was the first of his 26 Test caps. He scored 43 and 15 and England won by 288 runs. It was an unusual match in that fifteen players (eight from England and seven Springboks) made their Test debuts including two who had never even played first class cricket before: England's Audley Miller in his only Test and Springbok Joseph Willoughby who would only play in two matches himself.

THURSDAY 13 FEBRUARY 1975

MCC made his 114th and last Test appearance for England – against Australia at Melbourne Cricket Ground. Michael Colin Cowdrey had made his first appearance also against Australia (at Brisbane) on 26 November 1954 – 20 years, two months and 18 days earlier. He captained England 27 times between 1959 and 1968-1969, winning eight, drawing fifteen and losing four. In 1972 Cowdrey was appointed CBE, becoming Sir Colin in 1992 and Baron Cowdrey of Tonbridge, in the county of Kent in 1997, only the second cricketer to become a peer. In 1988 his son the Honourable Chris Cowdrey was asked by his godfather, Peter May, the chairman of England's selectors, to become England captain against West Indies. England were badly beaten and it was Cowdrey junior's last Test appearance.

SUNDAY 14 FEBRUARY 1971

England fast bowler John Snow hit Australian tail-ender Terry Jenner in the face with a bouncer at Sydney during the seventh Test. Umpire Lou Rowan told Snow to stop bowling bumpers, which led to a protest from England captain Ray Illingworth. Beer bottles were thrown at the England team and spectator Trevor Guy grabbed Snow as he fielded at the boundary so Illingworth took his players from the field. The umpires warned Illingworth that unless his team returned they would forfeit the match. They did return and won by 62 runs.

MONDAY 14 FEBRUARY 2000

South African fast bowler Tertius Bosch died at Westville, Natal exactly a month before his 34th birthday supposedly of the rare autoimmune disease Guillain-Barré syndrome after a long illness. He made a solitary Test appearance in the first post-apartheid match against West Indies in April 1992. He never represented his country again at that level because, it was said, that he was a gentle and shy man and lacked the killer instinct of a pace man. Eighteen months after his death, rumours began to surface that his death was not all that it seemed. He had hired a private detective to follow his wife, Karen-Anne, after he became suspicious she was sleeping with another man. Following his death Bosch's sister Rita van Wetten and brother Toon Bosch also hired a private investigator, Hennie Els, to examine the financial affairs of Bosch and the circumstances of his demise. The private eye discovered some financial irregularities as well as a second will which disinherited Bosch's widow, Karen-Anne. The discovery led to Bosch's body being exhumed. Details also came to light of an affair between Karen-Anne and lawyer Henry Selzer who was the executor of Bosch's first will. The affair came to an end but not before Selzer began to suffer the same symptoms as Bosch shortly before his death. No trace of poison was found in the autopsy although his body was re-exhumed in November 2004 and a second examination in February 2005 did find traces of poison. In 2003 a judge upheld Rita van Wetten's appeal to have the first will which left everything to Bosch's widow overturned.

MONDAY 15 FEBRUARY 1932

The shortest Test match ended despite it being scheduled as a timeless Test. South Africa won the toss at Melbourne Cricket Ground and decided to bat but were skittled out for just 36 with only captain-wicketkeeper Jock Cameron reaching double figures. Bert Ironmonger took 5 for 6 from 7.2 overs and his first victim brought up his fiftieth first class wicket and his second brought up his fiftieth Test wicket. Australia replied with 153 all out although Don Bradman was absent hurt. The Springboks collapsed again in their second innings making just 45 and only Syd Curnow reached double figures among the five ducks. Australia won by an innings and 72 runs but the players were only on the field for five hours and fifty-three minutes. The match also had the lowest total aggregate of runs in a complete Test – just 234 for the loss of 29 wickets while South Africa had the lowest total for losing all twenty wickets.

WEDNESDAY 15 FEBRUARY 1978

New Zealand beat England for the first time in a Test match – 48 years after the teams met for the first time. Played at the Basin Reserve, Wellington England captain Geoff Boycott won the toss and decided to field. The Kiwis made 228 with opener John Wright being the top scorer on his debut with 55. Chris Old took 6 for 54. In reply the tourists made 215 including a 77 from captain Boycott. Richard Hadlee took 4 for 74. Thanks to 5 for 32 from fast bowler Bob Willis England dismissed New Zealand for 123 and looked set for another victory. Hadlee had other ideas and tore through the England batting taking 6 for 26 as England collapsed to 64 all out and New Zealand won the match by 72 runs.

THURSDAY 16 FEBRUARY 1865

The first inter-colonial match in the West Indies ended. It was a contest between Barbados and Demerara. Barbados batted first and were all out for 74 with fast bowler George Whitehall the top scorer on 21. Only one other player reached double figures. Frederick Smith took six Demeraran wickets as they were all out for 22. Captain G.H. Oliver was the top scorer with eight runs closely followed by Extras on seven. Frederick Smith opened Barbados's second innings and hit the nation's first first class fifty (and was the first to carry his bat) as they made 124 and then picked up four more wickets as Demerara were all out for 38. Barbados enjoyed a sweet victory by 138 runs.

SUNDAY 16 FEBRUARY 1936

South African Test wicketkeeper Tommy Ward electrocuted aged 48 while working at the West Springs Gold Mine. He made his Test debut against Australia at Old Trafford, Manchester in 1912 and bagged a pair. Following his retirement, he worked in a mine.

MONDAY 17 FEBRUARY 1936

Leg break bowler Clarrie Grimmett became the first cricketer to take two hundred wickets in Test cricket. He achieved the feat at Old Wanderers, Johannesburg on the second and final day of the fourth Test for Australia against South Africa. Grimmett took 3 for 70 and 7 for 40 in what was to be his penultimate Test. Ironically, for such a stalwart of Australian Test cricket he was actually born in New Zealand.

THURSDAY 17 FEBRUARY 2005

Australia (214 for 5) beat New Zealand (170) by 44 runs in the first international Twenty20 match, played at Eden Park in Auckland in front of a 29,000 crowd. It was a light-hearted match. The Kiwi team wore kit identical to that of their supporters the Beige Brigade who had promised to deliver a crate of beer to the home club of any player sporting a real moustache. Glenn McGrath bowled an under-arm delivery in the final over, echoing the action of Trevor Chappell twenty-four years earlier (see 1 February 1981). The action resulted in umpire Billy Bowden producing a red card.

MONDAY 18 FEBRUARY 1924

New South Wales beat Otago by an innings and 327 runs at Carisbrook, Dunedin in the third match of their twelve game tour of New Zealand. Otago won the toss and decided to bat and made 261 with leg-break bowler Arthur Mailey taking 5 for 64. In their innings New South Wales made 752 for 8 declared – the highest innings total in a first class match in New Zealand – which included three centuries and three fifties. They then bowled Otago out for 164 with Mailey taking six more wickets (for 41) to bring his tally for the match to 11 for 105.

TUESDAY 18 FEBRUARY 1986

A delivery from West Indian pace man Malcolm Marshall at Sabina Park, Kingston broke the nose of England number four Mike Gatting in the first one day international when the batsman was on 10. To add insult to injury the ball bounced off Gatting's nose onto his wicket and dislodged the bails. And West Indies won the match.

FRIDAY 19 FEBRUARY 1915

Norman Callaway made his first class debut aged 18 for New South Wales at Sydney Cricket Ground against Queensland and by close of play was 125 not out. By the time he was out the next day, he had made 207 – to become the first man to score a double hundred on debut. He scored 26 fours during the 214-minute innings. It would also be his only first class appearance and he joined the army. He was killed during an attack on the Hindenburg Line (also known as the Siegfried Line) during the 2nd Battle of Bullecourt, France on 3 May 1917 while serving with the 19th NSW Battalion AIF. He was four weeks past his 21st birthday.

TUESDAY 19 FEBRUARY 1980

Ian Botham became the first man to score a century and take ten wickets in a Test match when he scored 114 and took 6 for 58 and 7 for 48 in the Golden Jubilee Test against India at Wankhede Stadium, Bombay.

FRIDAY 20 FEBRUARY 1959

Wicketkeeper Gerry Alexander became the last white man to captain West Indies when he led them in the first Test against Pakistan in Karachi. Alexander had made his Test debut under John Goddard at Headingley, Leeds in 1957 and played just two Tests before being given the captaincy. West Indies won seven, lost four and drew seven of his 18 Tests in charge.

TUESDAY 20 FEBRUARY 1990

In a bid to force a result in the Shell Trophy match between Wellington and Canterbury at Christchurch, Wellington's captain-wicketkeeper Erve McSweeney tossed the ball to batsman Bert Vance who was no bowler to deliver the penultimate over. Wellington needed to win the game to ensure that they won the Shell Trophy but Canterbury decided to play for a draw. McSweeney hoped that Vance's bowling would be so bad that they would get close to their total needed to win (291 from 59 overs) and thus risk their wickets and the match. At the start of the over Canterbury were 196 for 8 with captain Lee Germon on 75 not out. Vance began to bowl a series of no-balls, which were dispatched to the boundary by a grateful Germon who quickly reached his century and hit 70 including eight sixes and five fours off the over in total. At the other end Roger Ward scored five off the over. The scorers and scoreboard lost track of the score and began to ask the crowd for help. Even the umpire was puzzled and called over after five legitimate balls. Ewan Gray stepped up to bowl the final over but no one on either side knew that Canterbury were just 18 short of victory. Lee Germon hit 17 from the over but with the scoreboard out of action nobody seemed to know what was going on; Gray blocked the last ball rather than hitting one run needed to win.

FRIDAY 21 FEBRUARY 1930

The third Test began at Bourda, Georgetown, British Guiana between West Indies and England, which the home side won by 289 runs. Their victory was helped by George Headley who became the youngest Test player to score a century in both innings (114 and 112) – a record that stood until 8 March 2009 when it was broken by Phillip Hughes of Australia.

MONDAY 21 FEBRUARY 1972

Laurence Rowe became the first and so far only player to score a century in both innings of his Test debut – when he made 100 not out against New Zealand at Sabina Park, Kingston, Jamaica. Batting at number three, he made 214 in the first innings out of a West Indies total of 508 for 4 declared. In the second innings he made 100 without defeat. The match ended in a draw but Rowe was one of only two West Indies players who did not bowl in the match – the other being wicketkeeper Mike Findlay.

THURSDAY 22 FEBRUARY 1990

The England rebels led to South Africa by Mike Gatting played their last match on the tour – a 55-over match played at New Wanderers Stadium, Johannesburg. Kim Barnett scored 136 and Mike Gatting took 6 for 26 as England XI won by 134 runs. The freeing of Nelson Mandela from Robben Island Prison on 11 February 1990 disrupted the tour.

SATURDAY 22 FEBRUARY 1992

The fifth World Cup opened, the first to be held Down Under, with New Zealand 248-6 beating Australia 211 at Auckland by 37 runs and England 236-9 overcoming India 227 at Perth by 9 runs. For the first time the teams played in coloured kit with their names on the back and most of the 36 games were played under floodlights. Each game also used two white balls (one at each end) so they did not become too dirty.

SUNDAY 23 FEBRUARY 1992

A high-scoring match in the World Cup – 625 runs in 99 overs. Zimbabwe met Sri Lanka at Pukekura Park, New Plymouth and scored 312 for 4 off their fifty overs. Debutant Andy Flower carried his bat for 115 and Andy Waller was unbeaten on 83 when the innings closed. Zimbabwe's bowlers had Sri Lanka on the ropes at one stage when in the 39th over they were 213 for 5. Then Arjuna Ranatunga took matters into his hands and hit 88 in 61 balls to see Sri Lanka through to a three wicket victory with four balls to spare.

SUNDAY 23 FEBRUARY 2003

Opener John Davison of Canada scored a century in just 67 balls at SuperSport Park, Centurion – then the fastest ton in the World Cup but it was not enough to avoid a seven-wicket defeat at the hands of West Indies who took just 20.3 overs to knock off the required runs.

FRIDAY 24 FEBRUARY 1871

Six ball overs used for the first time in first class cricket when Victoria met Tasmania at Melbourne Cricket Ground. Tasmania won the toss and decided to bat making 103. Curtis Reid took 6 for 64. Victoria were bowled out for 129 before they dismissed Tasmania for 36. Needing just ten runs for victory, Victoria won by ten wickets on 11 for 0. Thirteen players made their first class debuts in the match including all the Tasmanian team apart from John Arthur.

TUESDAY 24 FEBRUARY 1953

Miles Giffard hanged at Bristol's Horfield Prison for the murder of his parents on the previous 7 November. His father, Charles, 53, was clerk of the court to St Austell magistrates and his mother, Elizabeth, vice chairperson of the St Austell Conservative Association and president of the Conservative Women's Association. Four years earlier, Giffard had played Minor Counties cricket for Cornwall and scored 89 runs in eight innings with a top score of 27.

TUESDAY 25 FEBRUARY 1975

New Zealand number eleven batsman Ewen Chatfield struck on the left side of the head by a bouncer by England fast bowler Peter Lever. Test debutant Chatfield collapsed, swallowing his tongue and only prompt medical action from MCC physiotherapist Bernard Thomas and ambulance man John May saved Chatfield's life. Thomas said that Chatfield's heart had stopped beating for several seconds: "It was the worst case I have seen and I never want to see another." Chatfield was carried off on a stretcher and an inconsolable Lever sat crying on the pitch. The injury to Chatfield forced him to retire hurt, which meant England won the match by an innings and 83 runs. Lever twice went to see Chatfield in hospital but on the first occasion Chatfield was still comatose. The second time the medium-pace bowler assured the pace man that it had not been his fault and that he had deflected the ball onto his own head. Lever later confessed that he thought he had killed Chatfield.

FRIDAY 26 FEBRUARY 1830

Civilians (76 and 136) beat 57th Regiment (101 and 87) by 24 runs in the first match in Australia for which team scores survive. At stake was £20 and around 100 people watched the match, the first time the number of spectators had been mentioned in Australia.

WEDNESDAY 26 FEBRUARY 1930

West Indies won their first Test match when they beat England. The occasion was the third Test of the 1929-30 series, held at Bourda, Georgetown, British Guiana and the Windies won the toss and elected to bat. They amassed 471 with a double century from Clifford Roach who had scored a ton in the first match between the two countries before getting a pair in the second before skittling England out for a meagre 145. A spirited fightback from England in their second innings was not enough to stop the home nation winning by 289 runs.

FRIDAY 26 FEBRUARY 1993

Australian Allan Border overtook Sunil Gavaskar to become the leading run scorer in Test match history. By the time of his retirement Border had scored 11,174 runs with a top score of 205 and an average of 50.56. As of March 2009, Border lies third in the all-time Test run scoring stakes.

FRIDAY 27 FEBRUARY 1925

Australian leg-spinner Clarrie Grimmett made his Test debut at Sydney Cricket Ground against England at the age of 33. Despite his relatively late start, he became the first bowler to take 200 Test wickets.

THURSDAY 27 FEBRUARY 1947

The oldest Test cricketer The Mackinnon of Mackinnon died aged 98 years and 324 days at his home, Drumduan, in Forres, Morayshire. The 35th Chief Of The Mackinnon Clan played for Kent. He is two years older than his nearest rival for the title of world's oldest Test cricketer – John Kerr of New Zealand who was a mere stripling of 96 when he died. The Mackinnon of Mackinnon played just one Test – in January 1879 against Australia. He was out first ball in the first innings (as one-third of Fred Spofforth's hat-trick – the first in Test cricket) and limped to five in the second. Australia won the match by ten wickets.

WEDNESDAY 28 FEBRUARY 1912

Australian opening batsman Victor Trumper's international career came to an end after 48 Tests in which he scored 3,163 runs. Frank Woolley caught him for 50 off Sydney Barnes's bowling on the seventh day of the eight-day fifth Test against England at Sydney Cricket Ground. To add insult to injury, England won the rubber by four Tests to one.

SATURDAY 28 FEBRUARY 1981

The second Test of England's tour of West Indies that should have begun today at Bourda, Georgetown, Guyana was cancelled because of seam bowler Robin Jackman. The Guyanese government objected to the fact that Jackman had played and coached in South Africa (he played for Western Province in South Africa in 1971-72, and for Rhodesia between 1972-73 and 1979-80) and deported him. The England tour party followed but Jackman made his Test debut in the third Test, which began at Kensington Oval, Bridgetown, Barbados, on 13 March 1981. Jackman took 3 for 65 in the first innings and 2 for 76 in the second scoring 7 in each knock with the bat.

THURSDAY 29 FEBRUARY 1996

In the World Cup the mighty West Indies were humbled by minnows Kenya at the Nehru Stadium, Pune, India. West Indies won the toss and decided to field and dismissed the East Africans for 166 – the highest scorer was Extras with 37 (10 leg byes, 13 no-balls and 14 wides). At one stage Kenya were 81 for 6 and part-time wicketkeeper Jimmy Adams made five dismissals. West Indies and probably all the spectators expected them to win with ease. The Windies progressed to 18 without loss and then the rout began – first to go was captain Richie Richardson losing his leg stump to Rajab Ali for five. When Brian Lara was out the Kenyans sensed blood and went in for the kill. Only Shiv Chanderpaul, Roger Harper and Extras reached double figures as the West Indians tumbled to 93 all out – their lowest World Cup total.

SUNDAY 29 FEBRUARY 2004

South African cricketer Lorrie Wilmot shot himself on his farm outside Grahamstown, aged 60. Wilmot would certainly have played Test cricket had it not been for his country's isolation from the sporting arena because of its government's policy of apartheid. He was selected to tour England in 1970 but when that tour was cancelled his opportunity for international sport was lost. Wilmot played 147 first-class matches in 28 years, captained Eastern Province and also played for Border. He scored 7,687 runs at an average of 32.02, a dozen centuries and a highest score of 222 not out. Estranged from his wife, in March 2003 he was convicted of raping a 13-year-old girl.

CRICKET
On This Day

MARCH

FRIDAY 1 MARCH 1839

Sussex CCC founded. Although the oldest county team, they did not win the County Championship until 2003.

TUESDAY 1 MARCH 1955

The fifth Test ended between Pakistan and India in a draw, as indeed had the previous four in the rubber – the first time all five Tests in a series had been drawn.

FRIDAY 2 MARCH 1984

Wicketkeeper Anil Dalpat became the first Hindu to play Test cricket for Pakistan. Playing against England at National Stadium, Karachi, he scored 12 and 16 not out and took one catch (to dismiss Allan Lamb). His Test career was quite brief lasting just nine matches.

MONDAY 2 MARCH 1998

West Indies beat England by 242 runs at Bourda, Georgetown in the fourth Test of the 1997-1998 rubber. It was the first Test match in which not one player was out bowled – twenty-nine were caught, ten lbw and one (Shivnarine Chanderpaul in the West Indians' second innings) was run out.

MONDAY 3 MARCH 2003

The World Cup match between South Africa and Sri Lanka at Kingsmead, Durban, ended in a tie even though the teams did not score the same amount of runs – thank to the Duckworth-Lewis method. Sri Lanka won the toss and decided to bat and made 268 for 9 in 210 minutes from their 50 overs. Opener Marvan Atapattu scored 124. Then the rain came and South Africa's total was reduced to 229 under the Duckworth-Lewis method. With Mark Boucher and Lance Klusener at the crease 12th man Nicky Boje came out to ensure that the two batsmen knew what was required but somehow the message was confused and the two batsmen thought that 229 was the figure needed to win when it was to tie. Boucher hit the penultimate ball for six and thought that he had just won the match so blocked the final ball rather than taking a single. The rains come down again and the match abandoned and the result declared a tie. Boucher's caution saw South Africa out of the World Cup they were hosting.

TUESDAY 3 MARCH 2009

The Sri Lanka Test team bus was attacked by a dozen terrorists as it drove to the Gaddafi Stadium in Lahore on the third day of the second Test against Pakistan. Captain Mahela Jayawardene, vice-captain Kumar Sangakkara and five other players, Ajantha Mendis, Thilan Samaraweera, Tharanga Paranavitana, Suranga Lakmal and Chaminda Vaas, and assistant coach Paul Farbrace received minor injuries, but six policemen and a' civilian driver were murdered in the assault, as gunmen targeted the wheels of the bus first and then the bus. "We all dived to the floor to take cover," Sangakkara said, "Thilan has a shrapnel wound in his leg, but he is fine. Paranavitana had shrapnel in his chest, but thank God it wasn't very deep and just on the surface. I had shrapnel injuries in my shoulder, but they have all been removed and I'm okay now. Ajantha had shrapnel in his neck and scalp, but he too has had medical attention and is fine. Everyone else is perfectly all right." The reserve umpire Ahsan Raza was also injured in the attack. The Sri Lanka team was evacuated and the Test abandoned. Ironically, they were only playing in Pakistan because India refused following the terror attack in Bombay in November 2008. The Test series was the first to be played in Pakistan since October 2007. Former Pakistan Test captain Imran Khan said, "This was one of the worst security failures in Pakistan. The government guaranteed they would provide them security. The security provided was shameful." On the first two days of the Test Sri Lanka had made 606, with Samaraweera making 214 before being run out, and Tillakaratne Dilshan 145 before he too was run out. In reply Pakistan had made 100 for 1 before the match was abandoned.

TUESDAY 4 MARCH 1958

West Indies beat Pakistan by an innings and 174 runs in the third Test at Sabina Park, Kingston, Jamaica to go two-up in the series. Pakistan won the toss and captain Abdul Kardar decided to bat. His side made 328 with opening batsman and wicketkeeper Imtiaz Ahmed scoring 122, Wallis Mathias 77 and Saaed Ahmed 52 while Eric Atkinson took 5 for 42. Then the whirlwind hit – Rohan Kanhai and Everton Weekes fell cheaply but opening batsman Conrad Hunte and Gary Sobers came together and put on 446 for the second wicket before Hunte was run out on 260. Sobers stayed at the crease for 10 hours and 14 minutes hitting an unbeaten 365 – then the highest Test score in the world – before the Windies declared at 790 for 3. With Nasim ul-Ghani (fractured thumb) and Mahmood Hussain (pulled thigh muscle) both absent hurt, Pakistan were all out for 288.

TUESDAY 4 MARCH 2008

Australian all-rounder Andrew Symonds floored a streaker who had the temerity to invade the pitch while the Warwickshire-born Aussie was batting in the second final against India of the Commonwealth Bank Series at Brisbane Cricket Ground, Woolloongabba, Brisbane. Symonds made 42 but India won by nine runs. Symonds, wearing number 63 and once considered good enough for a career in rugby league, shoulder charged the streaker when he invaded the pitch, with a policeman in pursuit, in the tenth over with the score at 34 for 3. The streaker, from Adelaide, was charged with disrupting the game and wilful obscene exposure. Another man tried to streak in the forty-second over but was stopped by security.

SATURDAY 5 MARCH 1977

England began their last overseas tour match under the colours of MCC – at Western Australia Cricket Association Ground, Perth against Western Australia. Apart from Tests the England team when touring abroad officially played as MCC until the 1976-1977 tour of Australia. Western Australia won the toss and decided to bat. Captained by wicketkeeper Rodney Marsh they made 326 for 8 declared with Craig Serjeant unbeaten on 101. In reply MCC scored 244 for 8 declared with opening batsman Mike Brearley top scoring on 61. Western Australia declared for a second time on 218 for 4 and by the time the match ended on 7 March MCC were 239 for 8. Bob Woolmer made 51 but when he reached 26 he passed 7,500 runs in first-class matches. The last time the England touring team wore the bacon-and-egg colours of MCC was on the 1996-1997 tour of New Zealand.

MONDAY 5 MARCH 1979

Terry Alderman bowled the last ball in the last Sheffield Shield match to feature eight ball overs at Western Australia Cricket Association Ground, Perth in a game between Western Australia and South Australia. Western Australia won the toss and decided to field. South Australia were bowled out for 107 with Bruce Yardley taking 5 for 27. Western Australia made 293 with Tony Mann making 84. Alderman took six South Australia wickets for 63 as Western Australia won by an innings and 41 runs.

WEDNESDAY 6 MARCH 1974

The third Test opened between England and West Indies at Kensington Oval, Bridgetown, Barbados. Fast bowler Andy Roberts made his debut for the Windies thus becoming the first Antiguan to play Test cricket. It was a match of firsts – Lawrence Rowe became the first West Indian to score a triple century (302) against England and all-rounder Tony Greig became the first England player to score a century and take 5 wickets in an innings of the same Test. The West Indians made 596 helped by a century from Alvin Kallicharran in a high-scoring match that saw England score 395 (Greig 148, Bernard Julien 5 for 57) and 277 for 7 (Keith Fletcher 129 not out) in the drawn game.

MONDAY 6 MARCH 2000

Mohammad Azharuddin played in his 99th and last Test (before allegations of match fixing ended his international career) and became the second batsman (after Australian Greg Chappell) to score a century in both his first and last Test matches. He scored 110 in his first match against England at Calcutta and 102 against South Africa at Bangalore (see 5 December 2000).

SATURDAY 7 MARCH 1987

India's opening batsman Sunil Gavaskar became the first cricketer to score 10,000 runs in Test cricket not long after tea in the fourth Test against Pakistan at Gujarat Stadium. He achieved the feat when he hit the ball for a two to take his score to 58. He was greeted by a crowd invasion that lasted for twenty minutes and obviously disturbed his concentration because, in his penultimate Test, he only added five more runs before Imran Khan had him lbw.

SUNDAY 7 MARCH 1999

Wajahatullah Wasti became the fifth Pakistani batsman to score a century in both innings of a Test match when he hit 133 and 121 not out at Gaddafi Stadium, Lahore in the third match against Sri Lanka of the Asian Test Championship. The game was also the one in which Wasim Akram became the first bowler from the subcontinent to take a Test hat-trick.

SATURDAY 8 MARCH 1873

New South Wales round-arm bowler George Moore became the oldest man to appear in first class cricket in Australia when he finished the New South Wales match against Victoria at Albert Ground, Sydney. He was 52 years and 334 days old. In Victoria's first innings his figures were 1 for 24 and in the second 3 for 17. In his first knock he was nought not out and in the second out for five. Victoria won by 24 runs.

SATURDAY 8 MARCH 1969

The third Test between Pakistan and England became the first to be abandoned, when the crowd rioted at lunch on the third day. England were 502 for 7; Alan Knott needed only four for a maiden Test century.

THURSDAY 9 MARCH 1916

Private Frederick Hardy of the County of London Yeomanry and former Somerset left-handed batsman and right-armed bowler was found dead in the Great Northern Railway gents at King's Cross station. His throat was cut and by his side was a bloodstained knife. Murder or suicide? Little information has ever been discovered although some historians believe that he killed himself rather than be sent back to the Western Front.

FRIDAY 9 MARCH 1945

Bombay beat Holkar in the final of the Ranji Trophy at Brabourne Stadium, Bombay. Holkar had imported a ringer in Denis Compton and a Bombay businessman promised him 20 rupees for every run he scored over a century. Bombay made 462 in the first innings although unusually not one player scored a century. Holkar replied with 360 but Compton made just 20. In their second innings Bombay scored 764 with one player hitting a century, another 151 and the captain Vijay Merchant 278. Holkar made 492 in their second innings but still lost by 374 runs. Compton made 249 not out but when he went to collect his money, all he found was a note that read, "Sorry, Mr Compton, I'm called away on very urgent business."

TUESDAY 10 MARCH 1970

South Africa beat Australia for the fourth time in the four-Test series that was to be their last international outing for 22 years, as they became outcasts of international sport. The Springboks won by 323 runs at Port Elizabeth. How good this team was will, sadly, never be known.

TUESDAY 10 MARCH 2009

England drew with West Indies in the fifth Test of The Wisden Trophy at Queen's Park Oval, Port-of-Spain, Trinidad and lost the series 1-0. England won the toss and chose to bat in a high-scoring match. The tourists declared at 546 for 6 with centuries from captain Andrew Strauss (142), Paul Collingwood (161) and wicketkeeper Matt Prior (131 not out). West Indies made 544 and also had three centurions: captain Chris Gayle (102), Shivnarine Chanderpaul (147 not out) and a maiden Test century from Australian-born Brendan Nash (109), one of the few white players to represent West Indies in recent years. England declared their second innings at 237 for 6 with 102 from Kevin Pietersen. West Indies chasing 240 were 114 for 8 when the match fizzled out into a draw. England wicketkeeper Prior set a world record of most byes conceded – 52 – in a Test match.

FRIDAY 11 MARCH 1910

England opener Jack Hobbs scored his maiden Test hundred – 187 against South Africa at Newlands, Cape Town. It was his 12th Test and the only one in which he was out hit wicket. England won by nine wickets.

TUESDAY 11 MARCH 1980

All eleven players bowled in a Test for the first time since 1884 – ninety-five years, six months and twenty-eight days. The first day and part of the second at the Iqbal Stadium, Faisalabad was washed out by rain and Australia then made 617 with captain Greg Chappell hitting 235 and future captain Graham Yallop 172. By the time the innings came to an end there were only seven hours and fifteen minutes of play left. In that time Pakistan made 382 for 2 and Chappell called upon all eleven players to bowl but only Geoff Dymock took a wicket (the other wicket was a run out). Greg Chappell took a turn behind the stumps as wicketkeeper as Rodney Marsh bowled ten overs including a maiden to end with figures of 0 for 51. It was the first time in any Test involving Pakistan that both captains scored centuries (Javed Miandad was 106 not out at close of play). Pakistan's wicketkeeper opened his side's innings and was 210 not out, meaning he was on the pitch for the entire match.

TUESDAY 12 MARCH 1889

The first Test match and the first first class match was played in South Africa between South Africa and England at St George's Park, Port Elizabeth. It was also the first time that England had been captained by a man playing his only Test and who also went on to become a successful Hollywood actor. Charles Aubrey Smith was a fine cricketer winning a Blue at Cambridge in 1882. That year he joined Sussex where he played for the next fourteen seasons, captaining the side from 1887 until 1889. In 1887-1888 he toured Australia winning 14 and losing two of the 25 fixtures and the following winter captained the first English side (Major Warton's) to venture to South Africa. The side won 13 and lost four of its 19 matches. On 12-13 March 1889 the tourists played South Africa at St George's Park, Port Elizabeth. This later became known as the first South African Test although it wasn't recognised as such at the time. In the Test Smith scored 3 and took 5 for 19 and 2 for 42 playing his part in England's victory. On the tour Smith took 134 wickets at a cost of 7.61 runs apiece. He stayed in South Africa after the tour to captain Transvaal against Kimberley in the first Currie Cup match on 5, 7-8 April 1890. A useful right arm fast bowler, his best bowling performances were taking 5 for 8 for Sussex against Cambridge in 1885 and 7 for 16 against MCC at Lord's in 1890. His highest innings was 142 for Sussex against Hampshire at Hove in 1888. He stood over six feet tall and had such a peculiar bowling action he was known as "Round The Corner Smith". He played 99 first-class matches for Sussex scoring 2,315 runs averaging 14.55 and taking 208 wickets for 5,006 runs averaging 24.06. A sporting all-rounder, he also played outside right at football for Old Carthusians and Corinthians. Following his retirement from the sporting arena, he moved into the theatrical one becoming an accomplished stage (début aged 30) and silent screen actor. In 1938 he was awarded the CBE becoming a knight six years later.

FRIDAY 12 MARCH 1982

The first unofficial "Test" began at New Wanderers Stadium, Johannesburg between South Africa and South African Breweries English XI captained by Graham Gooch and including Geoff Boycott, Wayne Larkins, Dennis Amiss, Bob Woolmer, Peter Willey, Derek Underwood, Alan Knott, Chris Old and John Lever. South Africa won the toss, decided to bat and made 400 for 7 declared. Jimmy Cook scored 114 and Peter Kirsten 84. In reply, SAB English XI were bowled out for 150 with Amiss hitting an undefeated 66 and captain Gooch 30. Top Springbok bowler was pace man Vintcent van der Bijl who took 5 for 25. Following on SAB English XI were all out for 283 with van der Bijl taking 5 for 79. Apart from Gooch who scored 109, no other player made more than 36. South Africa easily made their target and, at 37 for 2, won by eight wickets.

TUESDAY 13 MARCH 1956

New Zealand won a Test match for the first time when they beat West Indies in the fourth Test at Eden Park, Auckland by 190 runs. It was their first victory in twenty-six years and forty-five matches and followed three successive defeats in the rubber. The Kiwis captained by John Reid won the toss and chose to bat making 255 with Reid leading the way with 84. Tom Dewdney took 5 for 21. In their first innings the Windies made 145 (Hammond Furlonge 64, Tony MacGibbon 4 for 44, Harry Cave 4 for 22). New Zealand declared at 157 for 9 (captain Denis Atkinson 7 for 53) and then demolished the tourists, skittling them out for 77 (Cave 4 for 21) not long after tea on the fourth day.

THURSDAY 14 MARCH 1929

A day of records: when Jack Hobbs scored his 18th run in England's second innings against Australia at Melbourne Cricket Ground he became the first batsman to score 5,000 runs in Test cricket; at 46 years and 82 days he became the oldest batsman to score a century in Test cricket – it was also the first Test to be played over eight days and the game in which Hobbs scored his fifteenth Test century. It was also his last Test Down Under.

TUESDAY 14 MARCH 1939

The "timeless" Test between South Africa and England finally came to an end – after ten days (43 hours and 16 minutes), the longest first class match ever played and it only ended because the English tourists had to leave to catch the boat home. Beginning on 3 March South Africa won the toss and batted first. They made 530 all out with two centurions and three other players hitting half-centuries. England were dismissed for 316 with wicketkeeper Les Ames top scoring on 84. The Springboks made 481 setting England a target of 696 to win and they were just 42 short of victory when rain forced the match to be abandoned. Since there were 1,981 runs scored in the match it is surprising that there was only one double centurion (Bill Edrich who hit 219 in England's second innings) and five other hundred-makers.

THURSDAY 15 MARCH 1877

The first Test match began on a sunny autumn day at 1.05pm when 34-year-old Alfred Shaw of Nottinghamshire bowled to Charles Bannerman, a 25-year-old Kentish man playing his tenth first-class innings. Bannerman scored the first run in Test cricket off Shaw's second delivery. Before a forty-minute luncheon interval was taken at 2pm, Allen Hill bowled Nat Thompson for 1 to take the first Test wicket. Hill also took the first catch in Test history when he held T.P. Horan off Shaw's bowling. Bannerman scored the first Test century (taking 160 minutes) on the first day, which closed at 5pm with Australia on 166 for 6 with Bannerman not out on 126 and Blackham not out on 3. On the second day play began at 1.45pm and Bannerman retired hurt just after lunch on 165 having been at the crease for four hours and forty-five minutes, hitting eighteen fours. It was his only first class century. Australia were finally bowled out for 245 with Bannerman contributing 67 per cent of the runs, the highest individual contribution to any Test innings. No other Australian made more than 20. England made 196 before they skittled out Australia for 104. Despite needing just 154 for victory, England's second innings collapsed and they lost the match by 45 runs.

THURSDAY 15 MARCH 1979

In the first Test between Australia and Pakistan at the Melbourne Cricket Ground, the home side needed 382 to win and on the final day they were 305 for 3 when Pakistani captain Mushtaq Mohammad tossed the second new ball to paceman Sarfraz Nawaz. The Australians were unable to cope with his deliveries and Sarfraz took seven wickets for one run in 33 balls. Australia collapsed and were all out for 310 – Sarfraz took 9 for 86. Australia's number six to eleven made just one run between them.

WEDNESDAY 16 MARCH 1910

The only man to play Test cricket for England and India, the senior Nawab of Pataudi, Iftikhar Ali Khan, born at Pataudi, Punjab. Having won a Blue at Oxford, he was selected for the England squad for the 1932-1933 Bodyline series. He scored a century (102) on his Test debut but was dropped after the second Test after he criticised captain Douglas Jardine's tactics. He returned to England before his teammates. He played once more for England, also against Australia, in 1934 but then did not play Test cricket again until 1946 when he was captain of India for three matches against England. Apart from his first innings, he never managed to recapture his first class form on the Test arena and averaged only 19.90. His first class average was 48.61. He retired soon after through ill health and was only 41 when he died of a heart attack while playing polo.

SATURDAY 16 MARCH 2002

England beat New Zealand by 98 runs at Jade Stadium, Christchurch in the first Test. The tourists made 228 in their first innings with 106 coming from captain Nasser Hussain. The Kiwis were skittled out for 147 with Matthew Hoggard taking 7 for 63. An undefeated 200 from Graham Thorpe helped England to declare at 468 for 6. New Zealand then had to aim for 550 to win. It seemed an impossible task but Nathan Astle hit 222 from only 168 balls to take the Kiwis to within one hundred runs of victory. New Zealand were out for 451 – Andy Caddick took 6 for 122 – the highest fourth innings total by a team that lost the match.

SATURDAY 17 MARCH 1962

Charlie Griffith bowled to India Test captain Nari Contractor and struck him on the head. Griffith was already one of the most controversial fast bowlers of his and all time thanks to his bowling action. Today the Indian touring side met Barbados in a warm up game before the third Test at Kennington Oval, Bridgetown. Barbados had made 394 in their first innings with Erapalli Prasanna taking 4 for 158. The Indians went out to bat and lost an early wicket (Dilip Sardesai for a duck) when Contractor faced Griffith. Rusi Surti at the non-striker's end shouted, "Skipper, he's chucking." Contractor told his colleague to be quiet but perhaps the words had been more of a distraction than he thought as the ball from Griffith smacked into his head. With blood pouring from his ears and nose, the 28-year-old opening batsman was led from the pitch. When a doctor examined him, it became apparent that Contractor's skull was fractured and he had to undergo two emergency operations to remove clots from his brain. Contractor was comatose for six days and a number of players donated blood. Although after two years he recovered to play first class games, he was never to play Test cricket again.

THURSDAY 17 MARCH 1977

The centenary Test between Australia and England ended at 5.12pm and the result was the same as the first Test – a win for Australia by 45 runs. Australia had scored 138 and 419 for 9 declared with Chris Old taking 4 second innings wickets for 104 while England were skittled out for 95 in the first innings, captain Tony Greig top scoring with a meagre 18 as fast bowler Dennis Lillee took 6 for 26. In their second innings England made 417 all out with Derek Randall scoring 174 before being bowled by Lillee who took 5 for 139. Wicketkeeper Rod Marsh was the only other centurion hitting an undefeated 110.

WEDNESDAY 18 MARCH 1987

Viv Richards became the first player to score a century and take five wickets in a One Day International. West Indies scored 237 for 9 off their fifty overs and Richards hit 119. When New Zealand came into bat they were dismissed for 142 with King Viv taking 5 for 41 as the Windies won by 95 runs. (The feat would not be repeated until 21 June 2005 when Paul Collingwood scored 112 not out and took 6 for 31 against Bangladesh.)

SUNDAY 18 MARCH 2007

Pakistan manager Bob Woolmer died aged 58 in his hotel room at the Jamaica Pegasus Hotel in Kingston, Jamaica. His death came shortly after Pakistan had been dumped out of the World Cup by Ireland and four days later Jamaican police launched a murder investigation. Pathologist Dr Ere Seshaiah said that Woolmer had died of asphyxia via manual strangulation. Rumours immediately spread that the killer was a Pakistani angry at his country's exit from the cup tournament. However, on 12 June Lucius Thomas, the Jamaica Constabulary Force's commissioner, announced that Woolmer's death was due to natural causes and not foul play. However, an inquest jury after hearing 26 days of evidence returned an open verdict on 28 November 2007, thus not ruling out the strangulation theory.

TUESDAY 19 MARCH 1968

A tactical blunder by West Indies captain Gary Sobers let England win the fourth Test at Queen's Park Oval, Port of Spain by seven wickets and the series. West Indies won the toss and decided to bat and made 526 for 7 when Sobers declared. Seymour Nurse hit 136 and Rohan Kanhai 153 in the mammoth total. England replied with 404 all out with captain Colin

Cowdrey leading the way with 148. West Indies were then on 92 for 2 in their second innings when Sobers declared leaving England 215 to get in 2¾ hours at a run rate of less than four per over. Geoff Boycott hit 80 not out and Cowdrey 71 as the tourists reached the target.

THURSDAY 19 MARCH 1970

Opener Ian Redpath batting for Australia against Orange Free State in Bloemfontein scored 32 off one over – a record in South Africa. Facing Neil Rosendorff, Redpath hit 6, 6, 6, 6, 4, 4 and was finally out for 152. Rosendorff had his revenge; he dismissed Redpath, caught and bowled.

WEDNESDAY 20 MARCH 1751

The unloved Frederick Louis Prince of Wales died aged 44 leaving his younger brother George – later King George III – as heir to the throne. Fred disliked and was disliked by his own father George II whom he continually pestered for money. An abscess burst by a blow from a cricket ball brought about his death. A rhyme of the time summed up the public feeling:

"Here lies poor Fred who was alive and is dead,
Had it been his father I had much rather,
Had it been his sister nobody would have missed her,
Had it been his brother, still better than another,
Had it been the whole generation, so much better for the nation,
But since it is Fred who was alive and is dead,
There is no more to be said!"

MONDAY 20 MARCH 2000

Needing just 99 to win the first Test at Queen's Park Oval, Port-of-Spain, Trinidad – Jimmy Adams's first as captain – Zimbabwe collapsed from 47 for 3 to 63 all out. Only Grant Flower made a double figure score, and for the first time in 118 years a team had failed to reach a two-figure target to win a Test.

SATURDAY 21 MARCH 1992

Pakistan beat New Zealand in the World Cup semi-final. The Kiwis made 262 for 7 with Martin Crowe scoring 91 from 83 balls before his runner ran him out. Inzamam-ul-Haq made 60 off 37 balls and added 87 in ten overs with Javed Miandad before Chris Harris ran him out. With nine needed off eight balls Moin Khan hit Harris for six and then for a four.

SATURDAY 21 MARCH 1998

India inflicted Australia's heaviest post-war defeat – an innings and 219 runs at Eden Gardens, Calcutta. Australia were 1 for 2 after the first over and made 233 all out. India declared on 633 for 5 and the first six batsmen made 95, 97, 86, 79, 163 and 65. Shane Warne's figures were 0 for 147. Anil Kumble's 5 for 62 helped push Australia to 181 all out.

FRIDAY 22 MARCH 1985

Pakistani bowler Imran Khan took 6 for 14 in a One Day international against India at Sharjah Cricket Association Stadium, Sharjah, United Arab Emirates – and still ended up on the losing side. In the first match of the Rothmans Four-Nations Cup Pakistan won the toss and chose to field. Mohammad Azharuddin scored 47 but he, captain Kapil Dev (30) and Madan Lal (11) were the only players to make double figures as India were bowled out for 125. Pakistan were then dismissed for 87 and India won by 38 runs. For his pains – and the best bowling analysis for a losing side in an ODI – Imran was made man of the match.

SUNDAY 22 MARCH 1992

England played South Africa in a rain-affected World Cup semi-final at Sydney, Australia. The match was reduced to 45 overs and England scored 252 for 6 (Graeme Hick 83) off their allotted span. England had bowled 42.5 overs when it began to rain again and seventeen minutes of playing time was lost. When play resumed, the Springboks' target was revised to 252 from 43 overs, which meant that they needed to score 21 runs off one ball.

FRIDAY 23 MARCH 1962

The Nawab of Pataudi Jr became the youngest Test captain when he led India out for the third Test against West Indies at Kennington Oval, Bridgetown, Barbados. The previous captain Nari Contractor had had to withdraw from the match and indeed international cricket after a ball from fast bowler Charlie Griffith fractured his skull.

SUNDAY 23 MARCH 1980

Allan Border of Australia became the only batsman to score 150 or more in both innings of a Test match when having scored 153 at Gaddafi Stadium, Lahore in the second innings of the third Test he was stumped by captain and stand-in wicketkeeper Javed Miandad. In the first innings he was 150 not out in the match, which ended in a draw. The match was also unusual in that in Australia's first innings Pakistan used nine bowlers (all but wicketkeeper Taslim Arif and Azmat Rana) and ten in the second knock (everyone except Azmat Rana).

SUNDAY 24 MARCH 1611

On Easter Sunday, in Sidlesham, south of Chichester in Sussex, Richard Latter and Bartholomew Wyatt played "cricket" instead of going to church. They were arraigned by the churchwarden and then tried in Chichester Cathedral, found guilty and each fined a shilling.

SATURDAY 24 MARCH 1945

Spin bowler Sid Adams killed aged 40 while crossing the Rhine with the Allies. Leg spinner Adams had taken two wickets with his first two balls in first-class cricket playing for Northamptonshire against Dublin University in 1926. His first wicket was that of future Nobel Prize winner for literature Samuel Beckett.

TUESDAY 25 MARCH 1952

The only *Wisden* Cricketer of the Year who did not receive an obituary in the almanack Jack Newstead died at Blackburn, Lancashire, aged 74. Newstead was selected for the honour in 1909 after a spectacular season the year before for Yorkshire, when he took 140 wickets, at 16.50 each, and scored 927 runs. His form declined in 1910 and he was dropped but had there been a Test series in 1908 it is likely that he would have made at least one international appearance. *Wisden* rectified their earlier omission forty-two years later when Newstead appeared as a supplementary obituary in the 1994 almanack.

WEDNESDAY 25 MARCH 1992

Pakistan beat England by 22 runs at the Melbourne Cricket Ground to win the fifth World Cup. Pakistan won the toss and chose to bat first making 249 for 6 off their fifty overs. Captain Imran Khan top scored with 72 while Derek Pringle was England's most successful bowler taking 3 for 22. Captain Graham Gooch and all-rounder Ian Botham opened the England account but Botham fell for a duck with just six on the board. Neil Fairbrother topped England's scoring list with 62 but it was not enough and it was Imran Khan and not Gooch who held the trophy aloft.

SATURDAY 26 MARCH 2005

James and Hamish Marshall became the first identical twins to play Test cricket in the same side when they appeared for New Zealand against Australia at Eden Park, Auckland. Australia won by nine wickets.

THURSDAY 27 MARCH 1856

The first match between New South Wales and Victoria ended in victory for New South Wales (by three wickets). It was also the first match in which an innings was completed for a score of less than 30 when Victoria were bowled out for 28.

SUNDAY 27 MARCH 2005

Playing for Pakistan in the third Test against India in Bangalore, Shahid Afridi became the first opener to score 50 in fewer than thirty balls. Afridi reached 50 in 26 balls, hitting seven fours and two sixes along the way. He was finally stumped on 58 but Pakistan still won by 168 runs.

MONDAY 28 MARCH 1955

When a team scores 246 runs they normally do not expect to win the match by an innings but that is what happened today in the second Test between New Zealand and England at Eden Park, Auckland. The Kiwis won the toss and chose to bat, scoring 200. England began their innings on the second day (26 March) and by the time they were bowled out they had made 246 with Len Hutton in his last match for England hitting the top score of 53. New Zealand resumed but collapsed and were bowled out for just 26, which remains the lowest score in Test cricket ever. (The next lowest is 30 by South Africa on two occasions, both against England followed by 35 and 36 again by the Springboks and against England and Australia respectively.)

THURSDAY 28 MARCH 1968

Former Essex and England captain Nasser Hussain, OBE born at Madras, India. He played 96 Tests for England taking over as captain from Alec Stewart in July 1999. He averaged more than 37 and his top score was 207. However, not everyone was aware of him. In May 2005 Sir Bobby Robson was hired to promote Nobok sports legends and announced, "We've got a great list of cricketers joining us – Gary Sobers, Ian Botham, Graham Gooch, Alec Stewart, Mike Atherton, Saddam Hussein…"

FRIDAY 29 MARCH 1946

The first Test match after the Second World War was played between New Zealand and Australia over two days at Basin Reserve, Wellington. Australia fielded seven debutants while the Kiwis had six new players. New Zealand, captained by Walter Hadlee, won the toss and elected to bat but were no match for the Australians and were bowled out for just 42. Only two of the Kiwis made a double figure score. Tiger O'Reilly took 5 for 14 and Ernie Toshack 4 for 12 while Ray Lindwall took the remaining Kiwi wicket. When they batted Australia made just 199 with captain Bill Brown top scoring with 67 and Sid Barnes making 54. The most successful Kiwi bowler was Jack Cowie who took 6 for 40. When they resumed the match was over by 3.35pm on day two when New Zealand were all out for 54. Again, just two players scored double figures – this time five Australian bowlers shared the spoils as the Aussies won by an innings and 103 runs.

THURSDAY 29 MARCH 1979

Opener Andrew Hilditch became the first Test batsman to be given out for handling the ball in Australian first class cricket when he was dismissed in the second innings of the second Test against Pakistan at the Western Australia Cricket Association Ground, Perth. Nevertheless, Australia won the match by seven wickets.

SATURDAY 30 MARCH 1700

The first advertisement publicising a cricket match published in *The Post Boy*. It told "gentlemen, or others, who delight in cricket playing, that a match a cricket, of ten gentlemen on each side will be played on Clapham Common… on Easter Monday".

SATURDAY 31 MARCH 1877

The second Test began in Melbourne. Australia won the toss and elected to bat, making 122 all out. England replied with 261 before Australia hit 259 in their second innings. England made 122 for 6 to win by four wickets.

FRIDAY 31 MARCH 1978

West Indies played their first Test without the World Series Cricket rebels. Six debutants – Sylvester Clarke, David Murray, Basil Williams (who hit a century – exactly 100 – in the second innings), Alvin Greenidge, Norbert Phillip and Sew Shivnarine – lost at Bourda, Georgetown by three wickets.

CRICKET
On This Day

APRIL

SATURDAY 1 APRIL 1933

Wally Hammond scored an unbeaten 336 – then the highest Test score of all time – as England declared at 548 for 7 against New Zealand at Eden Park, Auckland. Having bowled the Kiwis out for 158 England made 548 runs in just two days – 61 per cent of the runs coming from Hammond's bat. New Zealand were 16 for 9 when the match ended in a draw.

THURSDAY 1 APRIL 1948

England lost to West Indies by ten wickets in the fourth Test at Sabina Park, Kingston. England failed to win a first-class match on the tour and skipper Gubby Allen was 45 years, 245 days – the oldest captain since W.G. Grace.

TUESDAY 2 APRIL 1889

Cricket writer extraordinaire Sir Neville Cardus was not born on this day despite claiming it as his birthday. He was actually born on 3 April 1888 at 4 Summer Place, Rusholme, Manchester. He never knew his father and his mother was a prostitute while his grandfather an ex-policeman. In December 1904 he became a marine insurance firm clerk and eight years later assistant cricket coach at Shrewsbury School in Shropshire. In 1914 he became secretary to the headmaster Cyril Alington, the future father-in-law of Sir Alec Douglas-Home, the only prime minister to play first class cricket. In 1916 he joined the *Manchester Guardian* where he became the newspaper's cricket and music correspondent. John Arlott wrote of Cardus, "Before him, cricket was reported... with him it was for the first time appreciated, felt, and imaginatively described."

SUNDAY 2 APRIL 1933

Ranji – Kumar Ranjitsinhji – died of heart failure in Vibha Villas, Jamnagar. He arrived at Cambridge in November 1889 having never played organised cricket before and later represented the university becoming the first Indian to win a Blue. He joined Sussex in 1895 and played for England the following year. He invented the leg glance and scored 62 and 154 not out on his Test debut causing one newspaper to report, "No man now living has ever seen finer batting than Ranjitsinhji showed us in this match". He never finished outside the top five in the batting averages between 1895 and 1904, when he stopped playing regular county cricket. He was appointed KCSI in 1917, GBE in 1919, and GCSI in 1923. His bedroom in Vibha Villas remains the same as it was the day he died.

SATURDAY 3 APRIL 1915

Beset by money worries, in failing health and with an unhappy marriage rugby and cricket international Andrew Stoddart shot himself in the head, aged 52 in a bedroom at his home, 115 Clifton Hill, St John's Wood, London. Born at 10 Wellington Terrace, Westoe, South Shields, Stoddart did not begin playing cricket until he was 22 in 1885 when he made his debut for Middlesex. He toured Australia four times (twice as captain including a winning tour in 1894-1895) and America and West Indies once each. In his fifteen-year career he scored 16,738 first class runs including 26 centuries. From 1886 until 1893 he took part in ten international rugby matches as a three-quarter. He played in 16 Tests for England scoring 996 runs, which included two centuries. *Punch* celebrated the Ashes win in 1894-1895 with a poem, which contained the lines:

> Then wrote the queen of England
> Whose hand is blessed by God
> I must do something handsome
> For my dear victorious Stod.

TUESDAY 3 APRIL 2001

Former Test player Javed Miandad sacked as coach of Pakistan following the country's poor performance on their tour of New Zealand and allegations of a rift involving senior players.

FRIDAY 4 APRIL 1930

Andy Sandham completed the first Test triple-century, shortly before the close of the second day of the fourth Test in Kingston against West Indies. Sandham ended the day on 309, and only managed to add 16 before being dismissed early the next morning for 325.

SATURDAY 5 APRIL 1902

Break O'Day and Wellington completed their single innings match to decide the championship of Tasmania. The match had begun a month earlier on 8 March but the authorities decided that no result could be confirmed until both teams had completed an innings. On the final day Charles Eady batted for eight hours and scored 566. His opposing captain Kenny Burn scored 121 – a rare event when between them the two skippers amassed 727 runs.

FRIDAY 5 APRIL 1974

Two Test giants bowed out. West Indians Rohan Kanhai and Gary Sobers both played their last games in the fifth Test against England at Queen's Park Oval, Port-of-Spain, Trinidad. England won the six-day Test by just 26 runs but on 30 March, the opening day, Sobers became the first West Indian to take 100 wickets when he dismissed Dennis Amiss for 44, caught ironically by Kanhai. Lance Gibbs became the second to achieve the feat when he clean bowled Geoff Boycott for 112 in England's second innings. Boycott had scored 99 in the first innings failing by just one run to become the first Englishman to score a century in both innings against West Indies. Kanhai scored a disappointing 2 and 7 but he did take a catch as wicketkeeper when Deryck Murray temporarily retired with a cut head.

FRIDAY 5 APRIL 1991

Mark and Steve Waugh became the first twins to appear in the same Test side when they represented Australia against West Indies at Queen's Park Oval, Trinidad. Mark Waugh top-scored with 64 in the first innings of a rain-affected draw, before taking his first Test wicket, Curtly Ambrose.

FRIDAY 6 APRIL 1877

Surrey's wicketkeeping bad boy Ted Pooley came to trial at Christchurch's Supreme Court having been on bail for four weeks. In 1876 he was picked to tour New Zealand and Australia. An injury forced him to miss a match so he travelled ahead to Christchurch, the venue of the next major match. He befriended a number of people and placed bets with them including one Ralph Donkin, a surveyor, who was staying in town. They wagered on how many men in the next match would score a duck. Pooley predicted eleven and reckoned to win £9 15s but Donkin refused to pay and the two men ended up scrapping. Pooley thought nothing more of it but as the team prepared to leave for Invercargill for their next game, Pooley and baggage handler Alfred Bramhall were arrested. Pooley was fined £5 but then Donkin accused him and Bramhall of vandalism and the magistrate ordered that they be bound over for trial. When the day in court arrived an important witness was missing and the jury returned a verdict of not guilty. He arrived in England on 9 July 1877, a month after the rest of the team. The greatest tragedy is that because of his actions Pooley spent time cooling his heels in New Zealand when he should have been playing for England in the first Test match. He never did get that England cap and died a broken man in 1907.

WEDNESDAY 6 APRIL 1977

Lintz Cricket Club of Burnopfield, Durham won a bid in the Appeal Court to lift a ban on them hitting sixes into a neighbouring garden. Lord Denning, Master of the Rolls, said that if John Miller, whose garden was "bombarded" with cricket balls did not like it, he should sell his house and move elsewhere. "For over 70 years the game of cricket has been played on this ground to the great benefit of the community as a whole, and to the injury of none," said the judge. Mr Miller and his wife, Brenda, had won a previous case banning the club from playing lest its balls land in his garden. Lord Denning said that if he was annoyed by the cricket he should go out or sit in the front garden or take up an offer from the club to fit unbreakable glass. "I expect there are many who would gladly buy it in order to be near the cricket field and open space," said Lord Denning. "At any rate, he ought not to be allowed to stop cricket from being played on this ground." The National Cricket Association and the Test and County Cricket Board underwrote the club's legal costs.

SATURDAY 7 APRIL 1962

West Indies beat India by seven wickets at Trinidad to win their fourth consecutive game in the series. Polly Umrigar scored an undefeated 172, the last of his dozen Test hundreds.

WEDNESDAY 7 APRIL 1965

New Zealand's Bev Congdon became only the second substitute to make a stumping in a Test match – he was the third to take the gloves in the second Test against Pakistan at Lahore. After Artie Dick was injured, captain John Reid took the gloves before handing them to Congdon. The match ended in a draw.

SATURDAY 8 APRIL 1882

Warwickshire CCC founded at the Regent Hotel, Leamington. The county won its first championship in 1911.

FRIDAY 8 APRIL 2005

New Zealand drew with Sri Lanka in the first Test at McLean Park, Napier. Lasith Malinga took 4 for 130 and 5 for 80 although the Kiwis blamed the umpire's trousers for his success. Kiwi captain Stephen Fleming said, "We asked the umpires to change the colour of their trousers. There's a period there [when it's a bit overcast] when it gets lost in their trousers."

SUNDAY 9 APRIL 1972

New Zealand openers Glenn Turner and Terry Jarvis put on 387 for the first wicket at Bourda, Georgetown, Guyana in the fourth Test between West Indies and the Kiwis. It remains the fourth-highest opening partnership in Test history. The match ended in a draw.

MONDAY 9 APRIL 1984

At Antigua Recreation Ground, St John's, Antigua West Indians Richie Richardson (154) and Viv Richards (178) added 308 for the third wicket against Australia; the home side went on to win by an innings and 36 runs.

TUESDAY 10 APRIL 1979

The last day of the last "Supertest" between WSC Australia and WSC West Indies ended in a draw at Antigua Recreation Ground, St John's, Antigua. WSC West Indies won the toss and chose to field. They dismissed the WSC tourists for 234 and despite a century from Greg Chappell seven players failed to get to double figures (Bruce Laird 2, David Hookes 2, Rodney Marsh 0, Ray Bright 0, Dennis Lillee 6, Jeff Thomson 4, Len Pascoe 8 not out). Colin Croft took 4 for 56 and Andy Roberts 4 for 73. WSC West Indies made 438 with Laurence Rowe top scoring with 135 and Lillee took 6 wickets for 125. When the match ended Australia were on 415 for 6 with wicketkeeper Marsh unbeaten on 102.

TUESDAY 10 APRIL 1990

On the last day of the Barbados Test England were destroyed by West Indian fast bowler Curtly Ambrose who took the last five wickets in 80 minutes with the second new ball. Ambrose returned his best Test figures of 8 for 45.

TUESDAY 11 APRIL 2000

Hansie Cronje sacked as South African captain after admitting that he had not been "entirely honest" when he denied allegations of match fixing revealed four days earlier by Delhi police. Three other players: Herschelle Gibbs, Nicky Boje and Pieter Strydom were also implicated. Cronje confessed to taking between $10,000 and $15,000 from a London-based bookmaker for "forecasting" results, not match fixing. Cronje revealed that he had been involved with dodgy dealing since 1996. On 28 August Gibbs and Henry Williams were suspended from playing international cricket for six months and fined R60,000 and R10,000 respectively. On 11 October

Cronje was banned from playing or coaching cricket for life. The Pretoria High Court dismissed an appeal on 17 October 2001.

MONDAY 11 APRIL 2005

Stephen Moreton had an inauspicious first class debut. Playing for Oxford University Centre of Cricketing Excellence against Gloucestershire at The University Parks, Oxford, captain Luke Parker tossed him the ball to bowl the last over of Gloucestershire's innings to New Zealander Craig Spearman who was on 182 not out. By the end of the over, Spearman was on 216 having hit Moreton for 34 (666646) – the most expensive maiden over in first class cricket.

SATURDAY 12 APRIL 1930

A timeless Test between West Indies and England at Sabina Park, Kingston, Jamaica, abandoned because of rain on the last two days before the tourists were due to sail home. The game, the fourth Test, had begun nine days earlier and England scored a mammoth 849 (Andy Sandham 325, Les Ames 149, Tommy Scott 5 for 266 from 80.2 overs) before bowling out the home side for 286. Despite a lead of 563, captain the Honourable Freddie Calthorpe decided not to enforce the follow-on and in the second innings England made 272 for 9 declared. The Windies were on 408 for 5 when the match ended. With it ended the longest Test career, that of Wilf Rhodes which had lasted 31 years, 315 days and aged 52 years 165 days.

MONDAY 12 APRIL 2004

West Indian captain Brian Lara completed his mammoth innings of 400 not out in the fourth Test against England – to regain the record for the highest individual Test innings that he had lost to Matthew Hayden earlier in the season. The West Indians declared on 751 for 5 as the Trinidadian left-hander faced 582 deliveries, hitting forty-three fours and four sixes, reaching the milestone just over two hours into the third day at Antigua Recreation Ground, St John's, Antigua. He survived an opportunity on 359 when Papua New Guinea-born debutant wicketkeeper Geraint Jones dropped what appeared to be a nick down the leg side. England were bowled out for 285 and the home side enforced the follow-on but a century from captain Michael Vaughan (140) ensured the match fizzled out into a draw.

FRIDAY 13 APRIL 1962

West Indies Test debutant Lester King took five wickets in his first four overs against India at Sabina Park, Jamaica. He finished with figures of 5 for 46 and took three more in the second innings as West Indies won by 123 runs. Despite early promise, King only played one more Test.

WEDNESDAY 13 APRIL 1994

England beat West Indies at Kensington Oval, Bridgetown, Barbados by 208 runs – the first time the home side had lost on that ground for 59 years. England made 355 including 118 from Alec Stewart. Windies made 304 with Angus Fraser taking 8 for 75. Michael Atherton declared on 394 for 7 with Stewart hitting 143, his second ton of the Test, which earned him the Man of the Match award. Courtney Walsh took 5 for 94. The home side needed 446 for victory but England dismissed the Windies for 237. Andy Caddick took 5 for 63.

THURSDAY 14 APRIL 1870

Australian captain Syd Gregory born at Moore Park, Randwick, Sydney, New South Wales (the site of the present Sydney Cricket Ground). Between 1890 and 1912, he played 58 Tests all but six against England. His highest score was 201 and he was *Wisden* Cricketer of the Year 1897.

SATURDAY 15 APRIL 1978

Sheik Faoud Ahamul Fasiel Bacchus made his Test debut for West Indies against Australia at Queen's Park Oval, Port-of-Spain, Trinidad. He made 9 and 7. Faoud Bacchus was to play in nineteen Tests for West Indies and every one of them was on a different Test ground.

WEDNESDAY 15 APRIL 2009

Former Zimbabwe Test player Andy Flower appointed England team director. He said, "Captains and coaches don't always have to agree or get on perfectly. In fact, it's healthy if there is always healthy debate between the two of you and the rest of the management team and squad. I respect Andrew [Strauss]. I think he's a very good cricketer and a very good captain." Flower, 40, played 63 Tests for Zimbabwe, the last in 2002.

FRIDAY 16 APRIL 1993

The first Test began at Queen's Park Oval, Port of Spain, Trinidad between West Indies and Pakistan. The home side collapsed to 127 all out from 63 for 0. Pakistan fared little better going from 100 for 2 to 113 for 7 and finally being all out for 140. Ian Bishop took 5 for 43. West Indies got their act together in the second innings scoring 382 and Desmond Haynes carried his bat for 143. Brian Lara was out for 96. Carl Hooper took 5 for 40 as Pakistan collapsed to 165 as West Indies won by 204 runs.

SATURDAY 16 APRIL 1994

The fifth Test began between West Indies and England at Antigua Recreation Ground, St John's, Antigua. West Indies won the toss and elected to bat but first blood went to England and the West Indians at one stage were 12 for 2 and then Brian Lara came to the crease. By the time he was out (the fifth wicket) he had scored the highest individual Test innings of all time – in 768 minutes he hit 45 fours and made 375, watched by the previous record holder Gary Sobers.

MONDAY 17 APRIL 1972

Sri Lanka's controversial off-spinner Muttiah Muralitharan born at Kandy. At the Melbourne Cricket Ground in 1995-1996 his career looked to be over as umpire Darrell Hair called him for throwing. Muralitharan fought back and took his 500th wicket in his 87th Test. In May 2004 he beat Courtney Walsh's record of 519 Test wickets and became the most successful wicket-taker in December 2007, going past Shane Warne's 708 wickets.

MONDAY 17 APRIL 1978

Having scored a Test career best of 65, West Indies off-spinner Derick Parry took 5 for 15 at Queen's Park Oval, Port-of-Spain, Trinidad as Australia collapsed to 94 all out. It was the only time that Parry took five wickets in a Test innings as West Indies won by 198 runs.

SATURDAY 18 APRIL 1992

South Africa returned to the Test arena in a one-off match against West Indies at Kensington Oval, Bridgetown, Barbados. Ten of the Springboks made their Test debuts – only captain Kepler Wessels had played before, albeit in Australian colours. After bowling out the home side for 262, the tourists made 345 with a maiden Test century (163) coming from Prince

Charles lookalike Andrew Hudson. He thus became the first South African to make a century on his first international appearance, a feat that was not repeated until Jacques Rudolph scored an undefeated 222 against Bangladesh in April 2003. Wessels made 59 while Jimmy Adams was the most successful West Indian bowler with 4 for 43. In their second innings the Windies hit 283 (Adams 79, Brian Lara 64) with Allan Donald taking 4 for 77 and Richard Snell 4 for 74. Despite 74 from captain Wessels and 52 from Peter Kirsten the might of Curtly Ambrose (6 for 34) and Courtney Walsh (4 for 31) saw off the South Africa side for 148. It was even made into a film although one review was obviously not written by a cricket fan: "In a play-by-play look at the final morning, the West Indies team defeats the South African team by an astonishing 52 runs."

SATURDAY 18 APRIL 2009

Bangalore Royal Challengers beat Rajasthan Royals by 75 runs in a Twenty20 match in the Indian Premier League held at the neutral ground of Newlands, Cape Town, South Africa. The Bangalore Royal Challengers, captained by England Test player Kevin Pietersen, won the toss and made 133 for 8 with Rahul Dravid hitting 66. Rajasthan Royals, captained by Australian spin maestro Shane Warne, were then bowled out for 58, the second-lowest total in Twenty20 history. Rajasthan lost their last five wickets for 11 runs. Anil Kumble took 5 for 5, the most economical analysis in Twenty20 competition.

SATURDAY 19 APRIL 1997

The first Test began between Sri Lanka and Pakistan at R. Premadasa Stadium, Colombo. Sri Lanka won the toss and chose to bat first making 330. Hashan Tillakaratne scored 103 and Saqlain Mushtaq took 5 for 89. Pakistan made 378; Ijaz Ahmed made 113 and Muttiah Muralitharan took 6 for 98. In Sri Lanka's second innings Aravinda de Silva hit 168. In his previous fifteen innings he had not made 40 but after this match he hit six consecutive Test centuries.

THURSDAY 19 APRIL 2007

West Indian cricketer Brian Lara announced his retirement from international cricket. He said that his last international game would be against England on 21 April 2007. It was a disappointing end – he was run out for 18 and England won the match by one wicket.

MONDAY 20 APRIL 1908

W.G. Grace began his 870th and last first class match captaining Gentlemen of England against Surrey at The Oval. It was not a great success as Surrey won by an innings and 41 runs. Grace opened the batting in both innings and scored 15 and 25. He bowled two overs at a cost of five runs. He was little short of three months before his 60th birthday. In 1,478 innings he had scored 54,211 runs at an average of 39.45 with a top score of 344.

FRIDAY 20 APRIL 2007

Former England cricketer Wayne Larkins and his girlfriend were given 12-month jail sentences, suspended for two years at Taunton Crown Court after pleading guilty to attempting to illegally obtain a mortgage secured against the house of her sick father. Larkins and Deborah Lines were also ordered to repay £54,000. Lines's father, 78-year-old Robert Adams, offered the couple a 50 per cent share in his Taunton home but Lines forged his signature to make it look as if she and Larkins owned the property outright. They then used that as security for a £155,000 loan to buy a home in France. Judge Graham Hume Jones said, "The fact is you were dishonest. Both of you were in this together."

WEDNESDAY 21 APRIL 1976

The fourth Test began between West Indies and India at Sabina Park, Kingston. The series was finely balanced at one all; West Indies won the toss and decided to field. India began solidly enough but then the West Indian pace attack began to hit home, literally. Anshuman Gaekwad retired hurt at 81 after being hit on the left ear by Michael Holding and had to spend two days in hospital as a result. Another wicket went down when Holding had Gundappa Viswanath caught at short leg and fractured his finger. Brijesh Patel deflected another Holding delivery into his own mouth and had to retire hurt. Bishen Bedi, the Indian captain, declared at 306 for 6 before any more of his men could be hurt. He also complained about the intimidatory bowling from the West Indians. The Windies made 391 although oddly not one player made a century – Bedi injured himself trying to catch Viv Richards and fellow spinner Bhagwat Chandrasekhar was also injured after he had taken 5 for 153. Substitute fielder Surinder Amanarth had to be hospitalised with appendicitis. When the Indians came to bat five players were absent hurt and the team collapsed to 97 when Bedi closed the innings. West Indies won the match by 10 wickets and the series 2-1 but during the match India had to call upon all seventeen members of its touring party.

TUESDAY 21 APRIL 1987

Richard Hadlee scored 151 against Sri Lanka at Colombo Cricket Club Ground – despite being known as an all-rounder it was one of only two first-class centuries the Kiwi hit. He took just 240 balls to score what was also New Zealand's 100th Test century. Hadlee's fast knock was in contrast to that of Sri Lankan opener Brendon Kuruppu who used up three days to score the slowest double hundred in first class history and finished on 201 not out.

MONDAY 22 APRIL 1867

An unusual match began in Islington, London. A team of one-armed men played a team of one-legged ones. The One Legs batted first and scored 89, with Birchmore top scoring on 46. The One Arms hit 143 with Redfern not out on 59. In their second innings the monopods scored 132 with Birchmore hitting 62. The One Arms made 59 for 9 as the match ended in a draw.

SUNDAY 22 APRIL 2001

South Africa dismissed West Indies in their second innings for 301 in the fifth Test at Sabina Park, Kingston. It was the first time in Test history in which all eleven players on the fielding side featured on the scorecard. It didn't help much – West Indies won by 130 runs.

FRIDAY 23 APRIL 1915

Cricket-playing poet Rupert Brooke died aged 27 of sepsis from an infected mosquito bite, off the island of Lemnos in the Aegean on his way to a battle at Gallipoli. In 1906 he played cricket for Rugby School and topped the bowling averages with 19 wickets at a cost of 14.05 runs each.

WEDNESDAY 23 APRIL 1986

Spin legend Jim Laker died aged 64 at Putney, London. At the end of his life Laker was a respected commentator for BBC TV but in 1960 he had had his membership of MCC and Surrey withdrawn after he painted an unflattering portrait in his badly ghost written autobiography *Over To Me*.

MONDAY 24 APRIL 1905

Jack Hobbs debuted for Surrey at The Oval against the Gentlemen of England captained by W.G. Grace. He scored the highest score in both innings of 18 and 88 – the first of 61,237 first-class runs, which included 199 centuries. In 1953 he became the first pro English cricketer to be knighted.

TUESDAY 24 APRIL 1979

The World Series Cricket ended when the Australian Cricket Board gave Kerry Packer exclusive rights to show their matches for ten years.

TUESDAY 25 APRIL 2006

Batting for British Universities against Sri Lankans at F.P. Fenner's Ground, Cambridge Richard Clinton made his side's top match score of 44 and was the last man out in the first innings. However, before he could bat again he had to visit a dentist for some emergency work as one of his teeth "imploded under the strain of furious gum-chewing".

TUESDAY 25 APRIL 2006

A group of Aussies commemorated Australia's war dead by playing a game of 22-a-side cricket on Tyagarah Beach at Byron Bay in the nude.

WEDNESDAY 26 APRIL 1972

Gary Sobers ended a run in the West Indies Test team of 85 consecutive Tests dating back to 11 April 1955 – a total of seventeen years and fifteen days. He had made his Test debut against England on 30 March 1954 but did not play again until the Test against Australia in April 1955. After the Test against New Zealand ended at Port-of-Spain he was not selected again until July 1973. Sobers played six Tests to bring his aggregate to 93 Tests.

TUESDAY 26 APRIL 1983

Australia beat Sri Lanka by an innings and 38 runs in the inaugural Test between the countries. Australia won the toss and decided to bat. They declared at 514 for 4 with Graham Yallop scoring 98 and David Hookes 143 not out (Hookes scored more than 100 runs in a session between lunch and tea on day 2). Sri Lanka made 271 all out (Arjuna Ranatunga 90 and captain Duleep Mendis 74) as Bruce Yardley took 5 for 88. Following on Sri Lanka made 205 and opener Sidath Wettimuny top scored on 96.

FRIDAY 27 APRIL 2001

Shoaib Akhtar of Pakistan became the first man to be recorded bowling at more than 100mph when his delivery hit 100.04mph during a one day international against New Zealand in Lahore. Craig McMillan was the batsman facing him down but the record was not recognised by the ICC because it could not agree on a method of measuring speeds.

SHOAIB AKHTAR BECAME THE FIRST 100MPH BOWLER IN APRIL 2001

SATURDAY 28 APRIL 1984

Clive Lloyd became the first West Indian to play 100 Tests in what was also the one hundredth Test to be played in the Caribbean.

MONDAY 28 APRIL 1997

The first Derbyshire cricketer to score a century on his first-class debut Ashley Harvey-Walker murdered in a Johannesburg bar, aged 52. He played for Warwickshire Second XI before moving to Derbyshire Second XI in 1967. He was 26 before he made his first class debut and was rarely sure of his place in the team. John Arlott once christened him Ashley Hearty-Whacker but he was sacked at the end of the 1978 season. Harvey-Walker was enjoying a drink at a private club in the Berea neighbourhood of Johannesburg, Transvaal when a man walked in and called out his name. When he responded, the man shot him dead.

SATURDAY 29 APRIL 1972

The first matches were played in the 55-over Benson & Hedges Cup in England. However, because of bad weather none were completed that day. In fact, it took three days to complete the one-day matches.

WEDNESDAY 30 APRIL 1975

Grey-haired bespectacled batsman David Steele played the first game of his benefit season. At FP Fenner's Ground, Cambridge against Cambridge University Steele scored 39 as Northamptonshire won by an innings and 31 runs. The financially astute Steele had made a deal with a Northampton butcher who offered him a lamb chop for every run he scored in his benefit season – at season end Steele had 1,756 chops in his freezer.

TUESDAY 30 APRIL 2002

Former Test umpire Steve Randell, 46, released from Hayes Prison Farm, north of Hobart after serving two years and nine months of a four-year sentence. Randell, the first umpire from Tasmania, officiated in 36 Test matches between 1984 and 1998 but was convicted in August 1999 on fifteen counts of indecently assaulting nine girls aged 11 and 12 while teaching at a Catholic junior school in Burnie in 1981 and 1982. Sentencing Randell, Justice Peter Underwood said that he was a serious paedophile who used his pupils as "sexual play things".

CRICKET
On This Day

MAY

SUNDAY 1 MAY 1949

The Board of Control for Cricket in Pakistan founded, two months after the team's first official overseas tour to Ceylon where they won both unofficial Test matches. Pakistan became an official Test-playing country on 28 July 1952.

WEDNESDAY 1 MAY 1963

The first game – a preliminary match – in the Gillette Cup took place between Lancashire and Leicestershire at Old Trafford. The match was held up for three hours by rain and so became the first to go over its allotted time. Peter Marner of Lancashire scored the first limited overs century (121) and took 3 for 49 which won him the first Man of the Match Award.

SUNDAY 2 MAY 1880

Australian all-round sportsman Tom Wills escaped from the Royal Melbourne Hospital where he had been admitted in an attempt to combat his rampant alcoholism. His grandfather had been a convict who had been deported to Australia. In his last years he had spent time in Kew Lunatic Asylum after claiming that aborigines were attacking his property. A day after his escape, he made his way to his home in Heidelberg where he stabbed himself to death with a pair of scissors. He was 44.

WEDNESDAY 2 MAY 1962

The first ball in limited overs cricket in England was bowled at Trent Bridge at 11am by John Cotton of Nottinghamshire to Mick Norman of Northamptonshire who became the first wicket and the first duck. At the same time across the Midlands Les Jackson of Derbyshire bowled to Maurice Hallam of Leicestershire who scored 88, the highest score until the first century was scored in the Gillette Cup the following year. It was the Midlands Knock-Out Competition (see 9 May 1962).

WEDNESDAY 3 MAY 1978

The fifth Test at Sabina Park, Kingston, Jamaica – Bobby Simpson's last Test – ended with a riot. Australia needed one more wicket with 38 balls left and when Van Holder was out caught behind by Steve Rixon the crowd invaded the pitch. The match was not finished because umpire Ralph Gosein refused to stand.

MONDAY 3 MAY 2004

Cricketing actor Anthony Ainley died aged 71. Perhaps because he relied on his face for his work, Ainley was careful when he played cricket and would go out to bat with pads, sunblock, helmet and a pair of swimming goggles.

SATURDAY 4 MAY 1963

Khalid Ibadulla became the last player in first class cricket in England to be given out handled the ball when he was dismissed for a duck playing for Warwickshire against Hampshire in the County Championship at Courtaulds Ground, Lockhurst Lane, Coventry.

SUNDAY 4 MAY 1969

Mike Denness and Brian Luckhurst of Kent became the first batsmen to share a partnership of 100 in a John Player League match when they put on 111 for the second wicket against Somerset at Bath.

MONDAY 5 MAY 2003

Australia beat West Indies at Kensington Oval, Barbados by nine wickets. Australia needed just eight runs to win but Jermaine Lawson captured the wicket of Justin Langer lbw to complete an unusual hat-trick – he had taken the wickets of Brett Lee and Stuart MacGill at the end of the first innings. He played just one more Test before the ICC questioned his action.

FRIDAY 5 MAY 2006

Shane Warne completed his rout of Middlesex, taking 7 for 99 at The Rose Bowl to lead Hampshire to a 10-wicket win in the County Championship. He confessed, "If I am honest, I'm tired out." Not surprising really when the night before he had been the subject of a newspaper sting when bitpart actress Emma Kearney rigged her bedroom with a video camera to catch Warne in flagrante with her and sexy model Coralie Eichholtz. Neither Warne nor Coralie were aware they were being filmed. Indeed, Coralie later admitted that had she known, she would have made herself look more glamorous.

TUESDAY 6 MAY 1676

The first recorded game of cricket outside the British Isles took place at the Green Plat, a valley four miles outside of Aleppo (in modern day Syria). Forty crew members of a ship, docked at the city, and the local consul enjoyed several games including "duck-hunting, fishing, shooting, hand-ball, krickett…"

MONDAY 6 MAY 1901

C.B. Fry scored just ten runs in his first match of the season, playing for London County against Surrey at The Oval. It was an inauspicious start to what was to be his best ever season. He scored 3,147 runs including a baker's dozen of centuries at an average of 78.67.

THURSDAY 7 MAY 1908

When a team scores 356 runs it normally does not expect to win by an innings and 314 runs but that's what happened to Yorkshire when they made their first visit to Northamptonshire in a game that began today. Yorkshire won the toss and decided to bat. They made 356 for 8 declared which included 110 from David Denton. Northamptonshire were missing three important players and bowler George Thompson was suffering from lumbago and unable to bat. Still, Yorkshire bowled out Northants for 27 in the first innings, George Hirst taking 6 for 12 and Schofield Haigh 3 for 11. Unsurprisingly, Yorkshire enforced the follow-on and this time dismissed Northants for just 15 with Hirst taking 6 for 7 and Haigh 3 for 8. The match was scheduled for three days but completed in two.

SATURDAY 7 MAY 1949

Cambridge University's John Dewes and Hubert Doggart added 429 for the second wicket – then the highest second-wicket partnership in English cricket – against Essex at F.P. Fenner's Ground, Cambridge as the university declared at 441 for 1. Essex made 304 for 9 declared before Cambridge declared their second innings at 142 for 3. Needing 280 to win Essex were 222 for 6 when the match ended in a draw.

TUESDAY 8 MAY 1923

Batting legend Jack Hobbs scored his hundredth first class hundred while playing for Surrey against Somerset at the Recreation Ground, Bath. Surrey won the toss and decided to bat and Hobbs was out for a duck as indeed was his opening partner Andy Sandham (who would achieve his own hundredth first class hundred on 26 June 1935). Surrey collapsed to 91 all out with Ernie Robson taking 6 for 59. Somerset did not fare much better being all out for 140. In their second innings when Hobbs achieved his milestone Surrey made 216 for 5 declared with an unbeaten 116 from Hobbs. Surrey then bowled Somerset out for 157 to win by just ten runs.

THE OVAL, WHERE IN MAY 1901 C B FRY MADE AN INAUSPICIOUS START TO A FINE SEASON

FRIDAY 8 MAY 2009

England beat West Indies by 10 wickets in the first Test at Lord's. The West Indians were replacements for Sri Lanka who could not muster a team because their top players would not leave the lucrative Indian Premier League. England took just three days to beat the Windies who had won the toss and elected to field. England were all out for 377, which included 143 from Ravi Bopara. Thanks to 5 for 38 from debutant Graham Onions the West Indians were bowled out for 152 and had to follow on. They made 256 leaving England 32 to make which they did exactly without loss.

THURSDAY 9 MAY 1872

An experimental game was played at Lord's between The First Eleven of MCC and Ground and The Next Twenty. The wickets were an inch higher, an inch wider and rather thicker than the usual 27 by 8 inches. The First Eleven of MCC and Ground batted first but the larger wickets did not seem to favour The Next Twenty – they only hit them twice as The First Eleven were dismissed for 99 with W.G. Grace top scoring on 41. The First Eleven had more success hitting the bigger wickets nine times as The Next Twenty made 46 – Alfred Shaw took 11 for 25. At 5.10pm when Shaw took the last wicket, it was decided to draw stumps for the day and retire to the pavilion and away from the bitterly cold wind that had bedevilled Lord's that day. The big wicket experiment was never repeated.

SUNDAY 9 MAY 1993

The Sunday league in England and Wales began its twenty-fifth season with a new sponsor and a few rule changes. The Axa Equity & Law League increased the overs from 40 to 50 much to the annoyance of the players, and introduced white balls and coloured clothing for the teams. The games also began at noon rather than after lunch, which befuddled some spectators. Umpires also wore blue coats and when Don Oslear took to the field for the first time he carried a crate of empty bottles and shouted, "Milko."

TUESDAY 10 MAY 1870

The first match of the 84th season of MCC was played between Right-Handers and Left-Handers. The southpaws batted first and were dismissed for 73 with James Lillywhite topping the scorecard with 26. Right-handed W.G. Grace took 6 wickets for 24 and then made 35 when he opened the batting. John Smith scored 45 to be the highest runs getter as the Right

Handers hit 185. For their second innings the southpaws were skittled out for 104. Harry Killick hit more than half to finish on 55 but it was not enough as the Right won by an innings and eight runs at 1pm on the second day.

SATURDAY 10 MAY 1958

Pakistani off-spinner and Lionel Richie lookalike Tauseef Ahmed born. He took seven wickets on his debut against Australia in 1979-1980, and took nine wickets against India in Bangalore in 1986-1987.

TUESDAY 11 MAY 1965

West Indies drew with Australia at Kensington Oval, Bridgetown, Barbados in the fourth Test of The Frank Worrell Trophy. It was the first match in which three players scored double centuries – a feat not repeated until Pakistan played Sri Lanka at Karachi in February 2009. Australia declared at 650 for 6 with Bill Lawry hitting 210, captain Bobby Simpson 201 and Bob Cowper 102. The West Indians were 573 all out which included 129 from Rohan Kanhai and 210 from Seymour Nurse. In their second knock the Aussies made 175 for 4 declared. The Windies needed 253 and were 242 for 5 when the six-day match ended. West Indies won the five-match series 2-0.

WEDNESDAY 11 MAY 2005

Spin bowler Shane Warne scored his maiden first class century batting for Hampshire against Kent and took just 72 balls to reach his ton.

MONDAY 12 MAY 1890

The first match in the County Championship began between Gloucestershire and Yorkshire at Ashley Down Ground, Bristol. Gloucestershire won the toss and decided to bat. Captained by W.G. Grace who opened the innings with his brother E.M. (who was out for the first duck, caught by Lord Hawke) the home county made 194, 101 of which were scored by Jimmie Cranston. Yorkshire were all out for 330 which included 107 from George Ulyett. In their second knock Gloucestershire made 178 and Yorkshire won by eight wickets after getting 43.

MONDAY 12 MAY 2003

Former England spin bowler Phil Tufnell crowned King of the Jungle in the ITV show *I'm A Celebrity… Get Me Out Of Here!* beating off the challenge of retired footballer John Fashanu and interior designer Linda Barker.

WEDNESDAY 13 MAY 1914

Reginald Erskine "Tip" Foster, the only man to captain England at football and cricket, died of diabetes aged 36 at his home in Brompton, London. *Wisden* Cricketer of the Year in 1901, he scored 287 at Sydney in 1903-04 on Test debut – the highest debut score and then-highest Test score. He became England cricket captain in 1907 for the rubber against South Africa but was unable to lead the winter tour to Australia due to business commitments. He played five football matches for England between 1900 and 1902, captaining the side in his last game against Wales, which ended 0-0.

SATURDAY 13 MAY 1972

Leicestershire became the first team to score 300 in a Benson & Hedges Cup innings when they hit 327 for 4 against Warwickshire at Coventry. Michael Norman and Brian Davison of Leicestershire became the first batsmen to share a 200 partnership – 227 for the third wicket.

TUESDAY 14 MAY 1872

MCC and Ground played The County of Surrey at Lord's with W.G. Grace opening the batting for MCC at 12.10pm. Forty-five minutes later, the entire team was back in the pavilion having been dismissed for 16 and at one stage were 0 for 7. The first runs went on the board and then another wicket fell and MCC stood at 2 for 8. There were eight ducks among MCC's batsmen. The County of Surrey began their innings at 1.10pm and by 2.30pm they, too, were back in the pavilion having been bowled out for 46. At 3.05pm Grace and Denzil Onslow opened MCC's second knock. They faced 77 overs and were dismissed for 71 at 5.30pm. The County of Surrey began their second innings at 5.45pm and at 6.40pm won the match by five wickets.

THURSDAY 14 MAY 2009

Ravi Bopara hit 108 against West Indies in the second Test at Riverside Ground, Durham – his third consecutive Test century, the first English batsman to achieve the feat since Graham Gooch in 1990.

SUNDAY 15 MAY 1966

Essex played Somerset in the County Championship at Ilford, the first time that a match in the tournament had taken place on the Sabbath. The law prevented Essex from charging for admission but the 6,000 spectators contributed £500 in collections and buying scorecards.

WEDNESDAY 16 MAY 1956

Bowling for Surrey against the touring Australians Jim Laker took all ten Aussie wickets conceding 88 runs. Spinner Tony Lock returned figures of 0 for 100. Ten weeks later, Laker again captured all ten wickets against Australia in the Old Trafford Test having taken nine in the first innings. That match Lock took the solitary remaining scalp. However, in the second innings of this match Lock took seven Australian wickets to Laker's two.

SATURDAY 16 MAY 2009

Former Indian captain Mohammad Azharuddin elected MP for Moradabad in western Uttar Pradesh, beating his nearest rival, Sarvesh Kumar Singh, by more than 50,000 votes.

MONDAY 17 MAY 1875

North played South at Lord's for the benefit of MCC Professional Fund. Unlike on most bank holidays, the sun shone on the crowd of more than 8,000 who travelled to Middlesex to watch the game. *Wisden* complained that there were too many people in the ground and – horrors – some sat in front of the scorers "render[ing] the perfect fulfilment of the scorers' duties next to an impossibility". North was missing many of its best players so its side had to be made up of local players. North won the toss and decided to bat. They made 90 with James Southerton taking 9 for 30. South made 123 and Fred Morley took 5 for 55. North made just 72 in their second innings which began at 5.12pm and was finished at 6.40pm. Southerton picked up seven more wickets at a cost of 22. W.G. Grace and Henry Jupp knocked off the 40 runs needed for a ten-wicket victory. It took eleven overs and fifteen minutes to hit 41 for 0. The match which had been scheduled for three days was completed in one.

TUESDAY 17 MAY 1955

Wisden obituary of West Indies fast bowler Leslie G. Hylton makes no mention of the nature of his demise, stating merely that he "died in Jamaica on May 17, 1955, aged 50". But Hylton didn't simply die; he was hanged for the murder of his wife Lurlene. Leslie George Hylton is the only Test cricketer to have been hanged for murder. A fast bowler, he was born on 29 March 1905 and made six appearances for West Indies between 1935 and 1939 and helped to win the rubber against R.E.S. Wyatt's touring side in 1934-1935 taking thirteen wickets in four

Tests at an average of 19.30. In 1939 he was not included in the side to visit England under R.S. Grant and a public appeal raised £400 to pay for his fare. It turned out to be a waste of money. He took just three wickets in two Tests. His top Test score was 19. He also played forty first-class matches for his native Jamaica, top scoring with 80 and taking 120 wickets. In 1954 50-year-old Hylton's wife Lurlene confessed to adultery with notorious womaniser Roy Francis. She said, "I'm in love with Roy. My body belongs to him," and pulled up her nightdress as if to prove it. He shot her seven times then phoned the police. At his trial his counsel produced a letter Lurlene had written to Roy Francis. "My beloved," it said, "I'm realising even more than I did before how much I love you. I am going to force my man's hand as soon as I can." He further claimed that Hylton was attempting to shoot himself but missed. Lack of accuracy was not the most credible defence for a former Test bowler with an average of 26.6, particularly given that he would have had to stop to reload his revolver, but it still took the all-male jury fully 90 minutes to convict. In his debut Test match against England in Barbados Hylton took three wickets for 8 in the first innings but despite this auspicious start his Test career lasted only six matches, ending in 1939. While in the death cell he was received into the Roman Catholic Church.

MONDAY 18 MAY 1885

Cambridge University played C.I. Thornton's England XI at F.P. Fenner's Ground, Cambridge. CI Thornton's England XI won the toss and decided to bat and were all out for 235. Cambridge University made 231 and John Crossland took seven wickets. CI Thornton's England XI were 165 for 9 in their second innings when the second day ended and rain put paid to the third day's play. It was only at the end of the first day's play that it was noticed that the pitch was actually 23 yards long.

THURSDAY 18 MAY 1905

Hedley Verity, one of England's greatest spin bowlers, born at Welton Grove, Headingley, Leeds, Yorkshire. A right hand batsman and left arm bowler, he made his Test debut against New Zealand at The Oval on 29 July 1931. In 1932 he took 10 for 10 for Yorkshire against Nottinghamshire at Headingley. He bagged a total of 15 wickets in the 1934 Lord's Test against Australia. He played his last first class match on 1 September 1939, for Yorkshire at Hove and took 7 Sussex wickets for nine runs in one innings.

THURSDAY 19 MAY 1842

The Honourable Frederick Ponsonby became the first recorded batsman to have scored nine runs from one ball while playing for MCC against Cambridge University at Parker's Piece, Cambridge.

TUESDAY 19 MAY 1903

In a fit of depression Arthur Shrewsbury of Nottingham shot himself at his sister's home in Gedling, Nottinghamshire. He was 47 and had only retired the year before. He was the first player to score 1,000 runs in Test cricket.

THURSDAY 20 MAY 1999

Ian Botham and Allan Lamb ended their legal battle against Imran Khan after costs spiralled out of control. At the end of the first trial in 1996 Botham faced an estimated legal bill of £260,000 and Lamb one for £140,000 and the judge said that proceedings were a "complete exercise in futility". The England Test players had sued Imran after he allegedly labelled them "racist, ill-educated and lacking in class" in an interview in June 1994 with *India Today* – a claim that the Pakistani all-rounder denied. A jury accepted by a majority of 10-2 Imran's claims that he had been misquoted and was only trying to defend himself after admitting that he once tampered with a ball in a county match.

MONDAY 21 MAY 1866

George Frederick Grace made his first class debut – a younger brother of Dr W.G. Grace, George was just 15 years and 159 days old when he played for the Gentlemen of England against Oxford University at Oxford to become the second youngest English first class cricketer.

SUNDAY 21 MAY 2000

England beat Zimbabwe by an innings and 209 runs at Lord's to record their biggest victory for 26 years. With West Indies also touring, it was the first time that seven Tests were played in England in a season. Zimbabwe were bowled out for 83 and at one stage they were 8 for 3. Ed Giddins took a Test career best 5 for 15 in his second international but within a month was dropped from the side and never returned. Thanks to centuries from Zimbabwe-born Graeme Hick and Alec Stewart England were 415 all out. Heath Streak took 6 for 87. Zimbabwe were all out for 123 in their second innings.

WEDNESDAY 22 MAY 1907

Bowler Albert Trott became the only man to take two hat-tricks in the same innings in a first class match in England. The game was his benefit match for Middlesex against Somerset and he went even further than two hat-tricks taking four wickets with four balls dismissing Talbot Lewis, Massey Poyntz, Sammy Woods and Ernie Robson (the first lbw the others all bowled). With his next delivery he dislodged the bail but in those days the rules stated that the bail must be removed for a wicket to be awarded. Later in the same innings he took the wickets of Osbert Mordaunt, wicketkeeper Archie Wickham and Albert Bailey (consecutively caught, bowled and caught). He also took two catches in the innings. Trott finished the innings with figures of 8-2-20-7. Middlesex won by 166 runs but Trott was said to have been seen punching himself in the head for finishing his benefit match early. To commemorate the event Sammy Woods gave Trott a straw hat with a hand painted band showing seven rabbits running into the pavilion.

THURSDAY 22 MAY 1947

In the summer in which he hit eighteen first-class centuries England batsman Denis Compton hit the first – and his victims were Worcestershire at Lord's. Compton finally made 112 – his eighteen centuries beat the previous record number, which was sixteen and held by Jack Hobbs in 1925. In 1947 Compton scored 3,816 runs with a top score of 246 and an average of 90.85.

TUESDAY 23 MAY 1899

Middlesex played Somerset in a match given over to benefit Wilfrid Flowers, the Nottinghamshire player and a member of MCC ground staff since 1878. The rain ruined the first day allotted to the match and no play was possible. Today the match was completed in just 185 minutes. It was the shortest completed first-class match but a disaster for the beneficiary. Somerset batted first and were all out for 35 with Sammy Woods who played Test cricket for Australia and England scoring 20 and Jack Hearne taking 5 for 14 (including three wickets in four balls). Middlesex were all out for 86 and Ted Tyler took 8 for 42. Somerset's second innings was slightly more successful and they made 44 with Albert Trott taking 7 for 13 (including three wickets in his first over) to add to the four wickets he took in the first knock.

THURSDAY 23 MAY 1918

Test batsman, Arsenal footballer and Brylcreem salesman Denis Compton born at 20 Alexandra Road, Hendon, Middlesex. He made his Test debut on 14 August 1937 against New Zealand. He won a League Championship medal and an FA Cup winner's medal with Arsenal in 1948 and 1950 respectively. He played twelve times for England during the Second World War but never played in a peacetime international. He played 78 Tests with a top score of 278. In 2005 the ECB and Cricket Australia decided to award the Compton-Miller Medal (also named for Keith Miller) to the Player of the Series in Ashes Tests. A popular cricketer, Compton was not always on top form between the wickets and had a tendency to run out his teammates. Middlesex teammate John Warr said of him, "He was the only player to call his partner for a run and wish him good luck at the same time." Trevor Bailey remarked that "a call for a run from Compton should be treated as no more than a basis for negotiation." At his brother Leslie's benefit match in 1955, he ran him out before he had faced a single ball.

THURSDAY 24 MAY 1877

Oxford University played MCC and Ground at the university's Magdalen College ground and found themselves bowled out for just 12 – the lowest ever total in first class cricket. Oxford won the toss and chose to bat. Captain Alexander Webbe did not arrive until lunchtime by which time his side had been in and were all out with only three players getting off the mark and Edward Wallington scoring seven of the dozen runs. It still took MCC 80 minutes and 43.2 four-ball overs to dismiss Oxford. Nottinghamshire left-arm fast bowler Fred Morley, who three years later opened the bowling for England in their first home Test, took 7 wickets for just 6 runs. MCC who were at one stage 93 for 2 collapsed and were all out for 124 with Henry Tylecote taking 8 for 51. Oxford's second innings was not much better – they were all out for 35 in less than an hour. Morley took 6 for 8, giving him match figures of 13 for 14. MCC won by an innings and 77 runs. The score remained the lowest ever until Northamptonshire equalled it in June 1907.

THURSDAY 24 MAY 1979

One of the shortest games on record of first class cricket lasted just eighteen minutes including the statutory 10-minute break between innings today. Worcestershire met Somerset in the Benson & Hedges Cup at New Road,

Worcester. Rain forced the game to be delayed by a day and Somerset would progress to the next round if they could manage to keep down Worcestershire's run rate even if the home side won. Consequently, after just one over Somerset captain Brian Rose declared on 1 for 0, the one coming from a no-ball from bowler Van Holder. It took Worcestershire ten balls to knock off the two runs, both scored by Glenn Turner. Charles Burnett, the Man-of-the-Match adjudicator, decided not to award it to anybody, explaining it would be "improper". Rose said, "I had no alternative. The rules are laid down in black and white. If anybody wishes to complain, they should do it to the people who make them." A week later, on 1 June, the TCCB expelled Somerset from the competition by 17 votes to one and later amended the rules to prevent declarations.

MONDAY 25 MAY 1868

The first overseas tour to England began. The team consisted entirely of Aborigines. Between May and 17 October they played 47 games winning 14, losing 14 and drawing 19. The tour was organised and the team captained and managed by former Middlesex and Surrey all-rounder Charles Lawrence. The tour uniform consisted of white flannels, red Garibaldi shirts with blue sashes and ties. As well as playing cricket, they were also called upon to demonstrate Aboriginal skills including spear and boomerang throwing as well as running, hurdling, the long jump and a water bucket-carrying race. The thirteen tourists were given nicknames to make them more acceptable to the English public. The nicknames included Peter (Arrahmunijarrimum), Sundown (Ballrinjarrimin), Tiger (Bonnibarngeet), King Cole (Brippokei), Jim Crow (Jallachmurrimin), Dick-a-Dick (Jungunjinanuke), Twopenny (Murrumgunarriman) and Mosquito (Grongarrong). The tour was arduous and only ten of the original thirteen completed it. King Cole died of tuberculosis in Guy's Hospital, London, on 24 June. Sundown and Jim Crow returned to Australia in August. Red Cap and Tiger played in all 47 matches.

SUNDAY 25 MAY 2003

Ryan Sidebottom played for Yorkshire against Glamorgan at Headingley in the National League and returned the bizarre figures of 0.1-0-11-0. The son of former Manchester United footballer and one-Test wonder Arnie, Sidebottom bowled two wides, was hit for six, delivered three more wides and then limped off with a hamstring injury.

MONDAY 26 MAY 1884

The Australians dismissed An Eleven of England in just four hours to win a match on a poor pitch at Aston Lower Grounds, Birmingham by four wickets. An Eleven of England won the toss and decided to bat but were all out for just 82. Fred Spofforth took 7 for 34. The Australians were then all out for 76, Percy McDonnell hitting 21 of their runs. Dick Barlow took 7 for 31. An Eleven of England then collapsed to 26 all out with Spofforth picking up another seven wickets at a cost of just three runs. The Australians' target was not high but they struggled and lost six wickets before they reached 33 runs. The match was scheduled for three days but completed in one.

FRIDAY 26 MAY 1916

Aboriginal fast bowler Jack Marsh died in hospital at Orange New South Wales, the day after he got into a fight in the street. He played just six first-class games taking 34 wickets with an innings best of 5 for 34. In November 1900 he clean bowled Victor Trumper. During a match with Victoria at Sydney in February 1901 umpire Bob Crockett no-balled 5ft 7in Marsh seventeen times for chucking although the other umpire allowed the delivery. Following his retirement from cricket, he took to the bottle but was a violent drunk. In 1909 he was sent to prison in Melbourne for assault. On 25 May 1916 he picked a fight with two men outside the billiards saloon of the Royal Hotel after he had been drinking heavily and he was violently assaulted. The assailants were charged with manslaughter but acquitted. A documentary film about Marsh was produced in 1987.

MONDAY 27 MAY 1878

Australians appeared at Lord's for the first time in a match against MCC who won the toss and decided to bat. The match didn't start until 12.03pm because of rain and W.G. Grace and Albert Hornby opened the batting for MCC. Grace hit the first ball for four and the crowd, which numbered almost 5,000, expected a good match. An eventful one was what they got. Grace was out second ball and then demon bowler Frederick Spofforth worked his way through the MCC side taking six wickets as they were all out for 33. Alfred Shaw took five Aussie wickets for 10 and Fred Morley five for 31 as the tourists were all out for 41. Shaw's figures were 33.2-25-10-5. When MCC batted again they collapsed to 19 all out with Spofforth taking four more wickets and Harry Boyle six. Nine of the ten wickets were out bowled. With just 12 runs needed, the Aussies made their target with the loss of just one wicket. The match scheduled for three days was over in less than one; 514 deliveries, 31 wickets and 103 runs.

SATURDAY 27 MAY 1905

Playing for Middlesex against Sussex at Lord's B.J.T. Bosanquet became the first player to score two centuries and take 10 wickets in a first class match. In the first innings he scored 103 and 100 not out in the second. With the ball he took 3 for 75 and 8 for 53 as Middlesex won by 324 runs.

TUESDAY 28 MAY 1912

Australian leg-spinner Jimmy Matthews took two hat-tricks in a Test match at Old Trafford, Manchester against South Africa. The Aussies, Springboks and England were taking part in a nine-match triangular tournament over a three-month period. The first match between Australia and South Africa began on 27 May and the Aussies were bowled out for 448. South Africa needed 298 to avoid the follow-on and seemed to be getting there, being 265 for 7 when Matthews was tossed the ball. A few minutes later, he had sent Rolland Beaumont, Sid Pegler and Tommy Ward back to the pavilion and the Springboks were all out with any addition to their total and were forced to follow on. South Africa slumped to 70 for 5 when Matthews was called upon to bowl. In this innings he took the wickets of Herbie Taylor, Reggie Schwarz and for the second time completing his trio of wickets with wicketkeeper Ward. Australia won by an innings and 88 runs early on the second day.

MONDAY 28 MAY 1934

Jack Hobbs scored his 197th and last first class century when he hit 116 while playing for Surrey against Lancashire at Old Trafford. At the time he was 51 years and 163 days old.

FRIDAY 29 MAY 1646

The first recorded game of cricket played on Coxheath, common land near Maidstone, Kent. It was the first contest in which all the participants were named and was a match between Thomas Harlackenden and Samuel Filmer against Walter Francklyn, Richard Marsh, William Cooper and Robert Saunders, all from Maidstone. It was also the first match on which a bet was placed. William Wood bet Nicholas Hunt a dozen candles that Harlackenden and Filmer would lose. The two beat the four but Wood reneged on his bet.

THURSDAY 29 MAY 1902

Edgbaston hosted its first Test match when England played Australia in the first game of the 1902 rubber. England, captained by Archie MacLaren and featuring C.B. Fry, Ranjitsinhji, the Honourable Stanley Jackson, Johnny Tyldesley, Dick Lilley, Gilbert Jessop and Wilf Rhodes, made 376. Australia were then bowled out for just 36 with only opener Victor Trumper scoring in double figures (18) and Rhodes taking 7 for 17. Enforcing the follow-on the rain stopped England winning the match and Australia were 46 for 2 when the match ended.

TUESDAY 30 MAY 1905

Archie MacLaren scored 140 for England in their second innings against Australia in the first Test of the five-match rubber. The century was MacLaren's fifth and the first to be scored at Trent Bridge, Nottingham. England finished by winning the match by 213 runs.

THURSDAY 30 MAY 1957

The first edition of *Test Match Special* began with the England v West Indies Test match at Edgbaston, Birmingham. The BBC advertised the new programme with the slogan, "Don't miss a ball. We broadcast them all." *TMS* began on the Third Programme before switching to the Light Programme at 5.15pm. As for the Test it ended as a draw with the most memorable event being a 411-run partnership between captain Peter May (285) and Colin Cowdrey (154) for the fourth wicket.

THURSDAY 31 MAY 1787

Marylebone Cricket Club formed with a match between Middlesex (with two of Berkshire and one of Kent) and Essex (with two given men) at Dorset Fields in Marylebone – the site of the modern Dorset Square.

THURSDAY 31 MAY 1923

Non-cricket loving monarch Prince Rainier III of Monaco was born. He was forced to play cricket while a pupil at Stowe. He remarked, "I didn't like it. It was the fielding I could not get used to."

CRICKET
On This Day

JUNE

SATURDAY 1 JUNE 1907

Epileptic left arm slow bowler Colin Blythe of Kent demolished Northamptonshire at County Ground, Northampton on the third day of the County Championship match. Kent had made 254 all out after rain washed out the entire second day's play. In 16 overs Blythe dismissed the entire Northants side for 60, his figures being 10 for 30. Kent enforced the follow-on and although Blythe could not repeat his performance in the second innings he still took a magnificent 7 for 18 to return match figures of 17 for 48. Ten years later, on 8 November 1917 Blythe was killed aged 38 by a shell blast on the Forest Hall to Pimmern military railway line near Passchendaele, Belgium while serving with the Kent Fortress Engineers. Of those who died in action, Blythe is the only Test player with a gravestone inscription referring to his cricketing prowess.

SATURDAY 1 JUNE 2002

Former Springbok cricket captain Hansie Cronje killed aged 32 when the Hawker Siddeley HS 748 turboprop cargo plane in which he was travelling crashed on Cradock Peak in the Outeniqua mountain range on its approach to his home town, George, in the Western Cape.

WEDNESDAY 2 JUNE 1880

Gentlemen of Canada's captain Thomas Dale arrested as he left the field at the end of the Leicestershire innings at Grace Road, Leicester in the second match of the Canadians' tour. He had played the first match under the alias Thomas Jordan and the reason became clear when Detective Crisp took him into custody on a charge of having deserted from the Royal Horse Guards Blues in 1873. Dale missed the rest of the tour as he was behind bars.

FRIDAY 2 JUNE 1967

West Indian paceman Roy Gilchrist became involved in an argument with his wife, Novlyn, about going to a party. He lost his temper, grabbed her by the throat with his left hand, pushed her against a wall, and branded her face with a hot iron. In August 1967 he appeared in court and was sentenced to a measly three months' probation. The judge said, "I hate to think English sport has sunk so far that brutes will be tolerated because they are good at games."

SATURDAY 3 JUNE 1899

England and Australia drew the first match of the first five-Test series. It was also the first Test to be played at Trent Bridge, Nottingham and was also Dr W.G. Grace's last match as captain and his last match for England. At 50 years and 320 days old when it ended he was the oldest Test captain. He was not the oldest Test player – that honour would go to Wilf Rhodes who ironically was making his Test debut in the match.

TUESDAY 3 JUNE 1975

Lancashire beat Derbyshire by an innings and 348 runs in a match at Park Road Ground, Buxton described by Dickie Bird as "nowt like I've ever seen". Lancashire won the toss, decided to bat and made 477 for 5 at declaration including centuries from Frank Hayes (104) and Clive Lloyd (167 not out). By stumps on the first day Derbyshire were 25 for 2. The second day was lost due to snow and then on the final day with an inch of snow on the pitch Derbyshire resumed their innings on the worst summer day of snow since 11 July 1888. Derbyshire tumbled to 42 all out with only two players making double figures. Following on Derbyshire more than doubled their score and made 87 with Peter Lever taking 5 for 16.

THURSDAY 4 JUNE 1970

A busy day for Yorkshire wicketkeeper David Bairstow – it was the second day of his first county championship game (against Gloucestershire at Park Avenue Cricket Ground, Bradford) but he also had to be up extra early so he could take his English Literature A-level at 7am. Later that day he held four catches but the match ended in defeat for the home side as Gloucestershire romped home by nine wickets – making their first county championship victory in the White Rose county since 1947.

FRIDAY 4 JUNE 1993

Shane Warne dismissed Mike Gatting with the "ball of the century", his first delivery against England in an Ashes Test. It was the first series in which England were able to select the players banned for a rebel tour to South Africa. Gatting, an experienced player of spin bowling, prepared to face Warne in his 12th Test. Unexpectedly, the ball spun more than Gatting anticipated and clipped the top of his off-stump, dislodging the bails. England captain Graham Gooch suggested, "If it had been a cheese roll, it would never have got past him."

THURSDAY 5 JUNE 1952

Len Hutton became the first professional England captain when he led the team out against India in the first Test at Headingley. India won the toss, elected to bat and made 293 all out with Jim Laker taking 4 for 39. England made 334 with Tom Graveney top scorer on 71. India then made history by losing their first four wickets without scoring in the first 14 deliveries.

MONDAY 5 JUNE 1972

Graham Saville became the first player to carry his bat through an entire Benson & Hedges Cup tie when he made 85 not out for Essex against Middlesex at Lord's. Middlesex won by 51 runs.

SATURDAY 6 JUNE 1891

The third and final day's play between Lancashire and Kent at Liverpool rained off as were the first and second days to become the first match in the County Championship to be completely lost to bad weather.

MONDAY 6 JUNE 1994

West Indian ace Brian Lara scored 501 not out for Warwickshire against Durham at Edgbaston as the county made 810 for 4, its record total in first class cricket. It was also the highest individual score for the county and came in the season that Lara equalled fellow Windies batsman Alvin Kallicharran's record of most centuries in a season – nine. Bizarrely, Lara was dropped on 18. Wicketkeeper Chris Scott said, "I hope he doesn't go on and get a hundred."

FRIDAY 7 JUNE 1957

Surrey's Micky Stewart took a remarkable seven catches in one innings against Northamptonshire in the County Championship. Stewart held six of the catches at backward short-leg and one in the gully. Tony Brown of Gloucestershire equalled Stewart's feat on 26 July 1966.

MONDAY 7 JUNE 1993

Playing against Australia at Old Trafford, England captain Graham Gooch became the fifth Test player to be given out "handled the ball". He was on 133 at the time and England lost the match by 179 runs. Gooch said, "It was an instinctive thing. I couldn't stop myself. If I'd had time to think about it I would have brought my bat up instead. I don't need reminding that we were looking like saving the Test when I got out."

MONDAY 8 JUNE 1857

James Grundy became the first player in first class cricket to be given out "handled the ball" while playing for MCC against Kent at Lord's. He had 15 on the board when he was given out. MCC won the match by five runs.

THURSDAY 8 JUNE 1950

West Indian spin twins Sonny Ramadhin and Alf Valentine made their international debuts in the first Test against England at Old Trafford. Valentine took 8 for 104 in the first innings, and 11 wickets in the match. England won by 202 runs but in the second Test (at Lord's) the spinners shared 18 wickets to inspire West Indies' first ever Test victory in England resulting in the *Victory Calypso* which began:

> Cricket lovely Cricket,
> At Lord's where I saw it;
> Cricket lovely Cricket,
> At Lord's where I saw it;
> Yardley tried his best
> But Goddard won the Test.
> They gave the crowd plenty fun;
> Second Test and West Indies won.
> Chorus: With those two little pals of mine
> Ramadhin and Valentine.

SATURDAY 9 JUNE 1934

So near and yet so far, Arthur Chipperfield made his Test debut for Australia against England at Trent Bridge, Nottingham – and scored 99 before being caught by Les Ames off Ken Farnes's bowling. He was the first player to be out for 99 on debut, having batted for three hours and 20 minutes. It was to be his highest score in the 1934 Ashes series. On 14 December 1935, he scored his maiden and only Test century (109) against South Africa at Durban.

MONDAY 9 JUNE 1988

England cricket captain Mike Gatting sacked after admitting that he took a woman back to his hotel room for a late evening drink. The Test & County Cricket Board accepted Gatting's denial of allegations in some national newspapers of late night sex romps with barmaid Louise Shipman but said that he nevertheless had behaved irresponsibly.

SATURDAY 10 JUNE 1899

Yorkshire beat Derbyshire by nine wickets at Dewsbury and Savile Ground in the County Championship. The match started normally on 8 June and Yorkshire made 343 in their first innings before an estimated 7,000 people. On the second day Derbyshire were bowled out for 203 with Wilf Rhodes picking up five wickets. Yorkshire enforced the follow-on and dismissed Derbyshire again for 171. After play finished on the second day the water in the pavilion was turned off at the mains for some work to be done. Unfortunately, a tap was left on in the canteen so when the water was restored at 6am the Derbyshire dressing room was flooded. The result was that their kit was awash and completely unwearable. So it came that on the last day with Yorkshire needing 32 to win the Derbyshire team – nine professionals and two amateurs – took to the field in their civvies. The two amateurs – Tom Higson who picked up one wicket and Levi Wright – bowled because they were the only ones with boots that could grip the grass.

MONDAY 10 JUNE 1991

England beat West Indies at home for the first time since 1969. They won by 115 runs at Headingley in the First Test. Graham Gooch scored an unbeaten 154; the first Englishman to carry his bat since Geoff Boycott in 1979-80.

TUESDAY 11 JUNE 1907

Speed cricket came to Spa Ground, Gloucester almost a hundred years before Twenty20. Gloucestershire played Northamptonshire and the first day (10 June) was ended by rain when Gloucestershire were 20 for 4. The second day, well day would be an exaggeration – in 260 minutes, the crowd saw 33 wickets fall for 180 runs. George Dennett bowling slow left arm for Gloucestershire took 15 for 21 and scored the only pair of the match. The game was abandoned as a draw at 4.30pm on the third day because of rain.

TUESDAY 11 JUNE 1946

Fast-medium bowler Peter Judge skittled out twice for nought inside a minute in separate innings. Batting at number eleven for Glamorgan against the Indian tourists, Judge was bowled first ball by Chandra Sarwate for a duck on the third and final day of the match. To save time, the Glamorgan captain Johnnie Clay forfeited the ten-minute break between innings and reversing his batting order instructed the last two batsmen to stay in the middle. Sarwate dismissed Judge again, this time second ball.

WEDNESDAY 12 JUNE 1895

Captain William Oates scored the first known triple century in Ireland when he hit 313 not out for 1st Royal Mounted Fusiliers against Army Service Corps at The Curragh. With Private F. Fitzgerald, Captain Oates put on 623 for the second wicket. The innings was finally declared at 658 for 1 – the first instance of a team scoring more than 600 in Ireland.

SATURDAY 12 JUNE 1926

A short Test match began eventually at Trent Bridge. Jack Hobbs and Herbert Sutcliffe opened the batting for England against Australia in the first of five Tests and reached 32 for 0 off 16.2 overs in fifty minutes before it began to rain again. There was no play on the second or third days and the match was abandoned as a draw. It was a similar result in the second, third and fourth Tests before England won the last Test by 289 runs to regain the Ashes.

THURSDAY 13 JUNE 1936

Playing for Gloucestershire against Somerset at Bristol Wally Hammond scored his hundredth first class hundred. In 1934 Hammond had averaged 122 but no one expected him to wait half a season before scoring his one thousand runs and this was also Gloucestershire's first win of the season – albeit a convincing one, by nine wickets. As with so many cricket matches in England, the rain had affected the pitch and Hammond took four hours to reach his ton – including seventy minutes to go from 81 to 100.

MONDAY 13 JUNE 2005

England (179 for 8) beat Australia (79) by 100 runs in the first Twenty20 international in England, played at the Rose Bowl, Hampshire. For a score of 34 and three catches Kevin Pietersen was made Man of the Match.

THURSDAY 14 JUNE 1984

Andy Lloyd made his Test debut for England against West Indies at Edgbaston, his home ground. Lloyd had done well in the One Day Internationals and was expected to replicate his form in the Test arena. Unfortunately, after he had scored ten and been in the middle for thirty-three minutes with the score on 20 for 0, Windies quick bowler Malcolm Marshall delivered a nasty ball that hit Lloyd on the temple of his helmet. Forced to retire hurt, he spent the rest of the match in hospital with blurred vision. He was unable to play again that year and was never selected for another international making him the only Test player to open the innings and never be out. To add insult to injury the West Indies scored 606 and won by an innings and 180 runs.

WEDNESDAY 15 JUNE 1960

Colin Cowdrey called the pitch at the Nevill Ground, Tunbridge Wells "disgraceful" as the County Championship match between Kent and Worcestershire was wrapped up inside a day – the first such occurrence since 1953. Kent batted first and made 187 all out with Peter Jones the top scorer with 73. Worcestershire then made 25 in 17.1 overs with no player getting out of single figures and six of them recording a duck. Alan Brown took 6 for 12. In their second knock Worcestershire more than doubled their score hitting 61 and David Halfyard taking 5 for 20 as Kent won by an innings and 101 runs.

SUNDAY 15 JUNE 1969

Greg Chappell became the first batsman to score a century in a John Player League match when he hit 128 not out for Somerset against Surrey at Ironmould Lane, Bristol. Somerset won the toss and decided to field. They were at 173 for 7 when their forty overs were completed. Wicketkeeper Roy Virgin and Chappell saw Somerset through to victory.

THURSDAY 16 JUNE 1932

A cricketing record nearly wasn't when dogged Yorkshiremen Percy Holmes and Herbert Sutcliffe made a first wicket stand of 555. When the White Rose captain immediately declared, pandemonium broke out. The scorers claimed that they had made a mistake and put the score back to the old record of 554. Luckily, a local vicar had been keeping score from the stand and he was able to correct the scorers.

THURSDAY 16 JUNE 1977

Mike Brearley captained England for the first time, after Tony Greig's involvement in Kerry Packer's cricket circus was revealed. Brearley led the team out at Lord's in the first Test of the Ashes. The match – the first of 31 in charge – was drawn but Brearley was on course to become the second most successful England captain of all time (after Douglas Jardine). Brearley won 18, drew nine and lost just four Tests; a success rate of 77.77 per cent. His batting ability was modest: he averaged 22 and never made a century.

FRIDAY 17 JUNE 1921

Cricket writer Neville Cardus married teacher Edith King. Legend has it that he went to the start of the Lancashire-Yorkshire match, left the ground to get married, and returned in time to see the pre-lunch overs. At about this time Cardus, who had always been known as Fred, adopted the name Neville, which alone appeared on his marriage certificate.

WEDNESDAY 17 JUNE 1970

Having cancelled the tour by South Africa on 22 May 1970, a hastily arranged replacement England versus a Rest of the World XI series began at Lord's. The game began on a Wednesday instead of the usual Thursday because Prime Minister Harold Wilson had called a General Election (he lost). Gary Sobers had agreed to captain the Rest of the World on condition the matches were given Test status. Geoff Boycott and Colin Cowdrey asked not to be considered for the match and when captain Ray Illingworth won the toss and chose to bat Alan Jones of Glamorgan and Brian Luckhurst of Kent opened England's account. Graham McKenzie bowled the first ball to Jones who hit it for a lucky boundary but after adding one more was out to a "rash, appalling stroke" the next over. At lunch England were 44 for 7, and by the end of the knock they were all out for 127. Sobers took 6 for 21. Rest of the World XI scored 546 thanks to 119 from Eddie Barlow and 183 from Sobers. In their second innings England were dismissed for 339 and Jones was out for 0. Intikhab Alam picked up 6 for 113. Rest of the World XI won by an innings and 80 runs. Alan Jones was never picked again for an international side and in July 1972 the ICC stripped the matches of Test status.

WEDNESDAY 18 JUNE 1975

Australia beat England by four wickets in the Prudential World Cup semi-final. Australia won the toss and decided to field and proceeded to bowl England out for 93 with seam bowler Gary Gilmour taking 6 for 14 in twelve overs and six maidens – in fact, he took the first six wickets as England collapsed to 36 for 6 before captain Mike Denness and bowler Geoff Arnold steadied things a little. It would not go all Australia's way and at one stage they were facing defeat at 39 for 6 until Gilmour came to the rescue with an unbeaten 28. Little surprise that game became known as "Gilmour's match".

WEDNESDAY 18 JUNE 1986

Cricket, a comedy musical based on the sport by Tim Rice and Andrew Lloyd Webber had its premiere at Windsor Castle as part of a celebration for the Queen's 60th birthday. Lasting 25 minutes, it was directed by Trevor Nunn and starred Ian Charleson, John Savident, and Sarah Payne. The musical had only two other performances although some of the music has since appeared in *Aspects of Love* and *Sunset Boulevard*.

SUNDAY 19 JUNE 1870

Popular Nottinghamshire batsman George Summers died at the tender age of just 25, four days after being struck on the head at Lord's by a quick delivery from John Platts, an MCC staffer. The pitch had not been properly prepared and the ball bounced around at head height from many deliveries. Summers was put in a carriage and taken over rough roads back home to his father's house in Nottingham where he died. Shaken by what had happened, Platt never bowled fast again and concentrated his efforts on medium pace where he achieved some success.

THURSDAY 19 JUNE 1980

England opener Graham Gooch scored his maiden Test century, having missed it four months earlier in Melbourne. Today playing at Lord's against West Indies in his 36th Test innings, he scored a magnificent 123 against an excellent Windies side. In fact, Gooch was responsible for almost 46 per cent of England's total of 269, which included fifteen extras. Five players failed to make double figures and when the tourists batted they made 518 with Des Haynes and Viv Richards, both playing their first Test at Lord's, scoring centuries. The Test was abandoned as a draw on the fifth day because of poor light.

FRIDAY 20 JUNE 1777

Hampshire beat England by an innings and 168 runs at Sevenoaks Vine Cricket Club Ground. After England were all out for 166, Hampshire scored 403 – the first known innings over 400 with 26-year-old opener James Aylward scoring 167, a new record individual score. John Wood picked up five wickets. England were dismissed for 69 in their second innings giving a commanding victory to Hampshire.

THURSDAY 20 JUNE 1878

W.G. Grace with his brother E.M. Grace and burly wicketkeeper Arthur Bush kidnapped all-rounder Billy Midwinter after he failed to show up for Gloucestershire's match against Surrey at The Oval. Midwinter who had been born in Gloucestershire but emigrated to Australia had that day intended to turn out for his adopted country at Lord's against Middlesex but Grace and his comrades jumped into a taxi to the home of cricket, burst into the visitors' dressing room and physically dragged Midwinter who was padded up and ready to bat with Alec Bannerman to Surrey's ground. When they arrived at The Oval the match had already began and Gloucestershire opted to field with a raft of substitute fielders. However, the Australians were furious at the turn of events and a number of them led by captain Dave Gregory bundled into their own cabs and drove to Kennington where they blocked Grace and co's entrance to the ground. Much shouting and fist waving ensued before Grace won, yelling at the bemused Australians, "You are a damned lot of sneaks." Unfortunately, Midwinter must have been unsettled by the to-do – he scored four and nought with the bat and took 4 for 65 with the ball as Gloucestershire lost by sixteen runs, their first defeat for two years. At Lord's, meanwhile, the Australians won by 98 runs.

SATURDAY 21 JUNE 1975

West Indies won the first World Cup at Lord's on midsummer's day against Australia. It was a close run thing and Windies batting first made 291 for 8 from their sixty overs with captain Clive Lloyd scoring 102. With the pace of Dennis Lillee, Jeff Thomson and Max Walker, it was Gary Gilmour who was the top wicket taker capturing five Windies scalps for 48. The Australians set off for their target with a vengeance but whenever they went for a quick single, so it seemed Viv Richards was always there to run them out. Five Australians lost their wickets that way, three fell victim to King Viv. Australia were on 233 for 9 and victory seemed assured for the Windies but last pair Thomson and Lillee had other ideas. Needing just eighteen runs for victory, at 8.42pm Thomson was run out by wicketkeeper Deryck Murray to give West Indies the honour of winning the first World Cup and £4,000 in prize money.

SUNDAY 21 JUNE 1992

All-rounder legend Ian Botham walked off a Test match pitch for the last time as a player. Botham had played the first of his 102 Tests against Australia at Trent Bridge in July 1977 when England beat the old enemy by seven wickets. Fourteen years, ten months and twenty-four days later, he was on the losing side as Pakistan won the match by two wickets. Botham made a disappointing two and six with the bat and only bowled five overs comprising three maidens, nought for nine. Botham scored fourteen Test centuries and twenty-two half-centuries. He took 383 wickets with a best of 8 for 34. Retiring from cricket in 1993, Botham was knighted in 2007.

TUESDAY 22 JUNE 1886

W.G. Grace became the only cricketer to score a century and take all 10 wickets in an innings in Britain since 1864. Playing for MCC against Oxford University at The University Parks, Oxford, Oxford University won the toss and decided to bat. They made 142 with captain Herbert Page top scoring with 49. At close of play on the first day MCC were 83 for 0 with Grace on 50. The Grand Old Man scored 104 before he was out leg before wicket and MCC finished on 260 all out. Oxford University made 90 with Grace taking all ten wickets at a cost of 49 runs. Four of his victims were bowled, four caught, one stumped and one lbw. MCC won by an innings and 28 runs.

SATURDAY 22 JUNE 1985

Comedian Rory Bremner under the pseudonym Commentators entered the UK pop charts with a song called 'N-N-N-Nineteen Not Out', a spoof on Paul Hardcastle's song 19 about the Vietnam War. Bremner, doing impressions of among others Brian Johnston, Richie Benaud, John Arlott, Bill Frindall and Jim Laker, referred to the Bodyline series and England's disastrous 1984 series against West Indies.

SATURDAY 23 JUNE 1928

West Indies played their first Test match. The game was at Lord's against England and the home side scored 382 runs on the first day finally reaching 401. Ernest Tyldesley, in his first appearance in a Test at Lord's, scored 122 and Learie Constantine took 4 for 82. The tourists made 177 with opening batsman Freddie Martin and wicketkeeper and captain Karl Nunes taking honours as top scorers hitting 44 and 37 respectively. Vallance Jupp was England's bowling ace taking 4 for 37. Fast bowler Harold Larwood missed the Windies second innings because of a strain but even without him England wrapped up an innings victory before lunch on the final day skittling out West Indies for 166.

SATURDAY 23 JUNE 1979

West Indies (286 for 9) beat England (194) by 92 runs at Lord's to win the second World Cup – and £10,000 in prize money. The victory was due in no small part to West Indian Collis King who hit 86 from just 66 balls.

THURSDAY 24 JUNE 1965

Former England captain Ted Dexter was driving his Jaguar home when the car broke down on the Great West Road in Brentford, Middlesex. He soon discovered the problem – he had run out of petrol. Dexter was either not a member of the AA or RAC or he had forgotten their telephone numbers so he decided to push the car to the nearest garage. Sadly for Lord Ted, as he was doing so he lost control of the Jag and it ran out of control pinning him to the gate of a factory, breaking his right leg in the process. It virtually wrecked his career.

MONDAY 24 JUNE 1996

Umpire Dickie Bird left the Test arena for the sixty-sixth and last time. His last Test was England v India at Lord's and at the start of the game the two teams formed a guard of honour as he came out, and he received a standing ovation from the crowd. Bird burst into tears.

MONDAY 25 JUNE 1934

Yorkshire spinner Hedley Verity took the record number of Test wickets in a day when he captured fourteen Australian victims at Lord's – to inflict the Aussies' first defeat (by an innings and 38 runs) at Lord's since 1896. In Australia's first innings Verity took 7 for 61 and in their second he took 8 for 43. The match was scheduled for four days but thanks to Verity it was completed in three.

TUESDAY 25 JUNE 1963

Which Test player began an innings as a righthander and finished as a lefthander? The answer occurred in the second Test between England and West Indies that ended in a draw today at Lord's. West Indies won the toss and decided to bat and made 301 and England responded with 297. Fred Trueman took 5 for 52 as West Indies made 229 all out. England were 116 for 3 when stumps were drawn on the fourth day, Cowdrey having retired hurt on 19 when England were 72 for 3. Brian Close batted heroically to make 70 as he was battered and bruised by the West Indian fast bowlers Wes Hall and Charlie Griffith. At 219 for 8 England needed fifteen to win and Cowdrey practised batting lefthanded in the dressing room. By the time Hall began to bowl the last over of the match to Derek Shackleton, in his first Test for eleven years, England needed eight to win. Shackleton swung and missed. He scored a single off the next delivery and spinner David Allen took guard – he hit a single and Shackleton faced the fourth ball and was run out. Cowdrey returned to the fray, his left arm in plaster and six runs needed for victory. Allen faced the last two deliveries and played a straight bat to ensure the draw.

SATURDAY 26 JUNE 1937

In an unusual situation both of England's opening batsmen Jim Parks and Len Hutton made their Test debuts in the first match against New Zealand at Lord's. Parks made 22 and 7, both times being clean bowled by Jack Cowie, also ironically making his first appearance for the Kiwis. Hutton fared worse scoring 0 and 1. Parks was never chosen to play for England again while Hutton went to on appear in 78 more Tests and add another 6,970 runs to his career total. Another debutant in the match was Walter Hadlee, father of future Test cricketers Sir Richard and Dayle and One Day Internationaller Barry Hadlee.

TUESDAY 26 JUNE 1990

The first Test of the England-India summer series began at Lord's. India won the toss and elected to field. It was to be a costly mistake – England captain Graham Gooch was in fine run-scoring form and in 627 minutes he reached his highest score in Test cricket: 333 from 485 balls which included three sixes and forty-three fours. It was the sixth highest ever Test score and the highest ever score at the home of cricket. Allan Lamb and Robin Smith added to India's misery as they also made centuries as England reached 653 for 4, the highest score against India. When they batted India made 454 avoiding the follow-on by one run – Ravi Shastri scored a century but it was Kapil Dev who got the necessary runs by hitting Eddie Hemmings for four consecutive sixes. In England's second innings Gooch scored another ton finally being out for 123 (148 minutes in 113 balls) to aggregate 456 – the highest ever in Tests and the second highest in first class cricket. Gooch declared on 272 for 4 and saw his bowlers skittle out India for 224 to win the match by 247 runs.

TUESDAY 27 JUNE 1899

Batting for Clarke's House against North Town in a junior house match at Clifton College in Bristol, A.E.J. (Arthur Edward Jeune) Collins completed a mammoth innings of 628 not out – the highest individual innings of all time. He batted for six hours and fifty minutes over four afternoons beginning on 22 June as his side made 836. The second highest score was "Extras" on 46 and naturally Collins carried his bat. The scorer, Edward Peglar, marked him down as "628 – plus or minus 20, shall we say". The knock was made up of one six, four fives, 31 fours, 33 threes, 146 twos and 87 singles. He was not just a useful batsman as he took 7 for 33 as North Town tumbled to 87 all out. Forced to follow on, North Town collapsed to 61 all out and Collins picked up 4 more wickets for 30 runs. The rather one-sided match saw Clarke's House victorious by an innings and 688 runs. It could have been so different – he was dropped on 80, 100, 140, 400, 556, 605 and 619. Rather than becoming a first-class cricketer, Collins joined the Army in 1902. He was killed in action aged 29, on 11 November 1914 at the First Battle of Ypres, while serving with the 5th Field Company, Royal Engineers.

SATURDAY 27 JUNE 1931

New Zealand played their first Test match abroad – at Lord's against England. New Zealand won the toss and decided to bat and the Kiwis were all out for 224 with Stewie Dempster making their first overseas half-century. Scottish born bowler Ian Peebles took 5 for 77. England made 454 with 137 from Les Ames. In their second innings the Kiwis made 469 for 9 declared with Dempster and Curly Page both making centuries. England were 146 for 5 when the match ended in a draw. After New Zealand's excellent performances in the first Test and county matches to that time, Surrey and Lancashire consented to drop their planned fixtures, and to make The Oval and Old Trafford available for two more Tests.

MONDAY 28 JUNE 1773

The first recorded instance of an attacking field took place in a match between England and Hampshire at Sevenoaks Vine Cricket Club Ground. Hampshire made 77 in their first innings while England made 177 including 73 from Richard Miller. In their second innings Hampshire were all out for 49 but England opener Richard Simmons was told to field close in and so "greatly intimidated the Hampshire gentlemen". It worked as England won by an innings and 51 runs.

MONDAY 28 JUNE 1915

Australia's leading opening batsman of the first decade of the Twentieth Century Victor Trumper died aged just 37 of Bright's disease at Darlinghurst, Sydney, New South Wales. It was just 3 years and 4 months after he had played his last Test match. Trumper made his first class debut in 1894-1895 and played in his first Test five years later on 1 June 1899. He played 48 Tests and 255 first class games scoring 16,939 runs with a top score of 300 not out. In poor health for some time before his death, a benefit match between New South Wales and a Rest of Australia XI at Sydney on 7-11 February 1913 raised £2,950 13s 3d. Buried in the Anglican section of Waverley cemetery, Sarah Ann Briggs, his wife (d.1963), a 9-year-old daughter Ann Louise, and a 16-month-old son, Victor Jr survived him.

WEDNESDAY 29 JUNE 1709

The first recorded game of cricket took place between Kent and Surrey at Dartford Brent, Kent, although no scorecard exists as to the complete result.

MONDAY 30 JUNE 1924

England scored a remarkable 503 runs in one day, during the Lord's Test against South Africa. England began the day on 28 for 0 after the Springboks had made 273 all out on day one of the second Test. Jack Hobbs made 211 (199 today) while Herbert Sutcliffe hit 122 (110 today) and Frank Woolley 134 not out with Patsy Hendren contributing a half-century. England captain Arthur Gilligan declared on 531 for 2 with one hour and six minutes to play before stumps were drawn. By close of play South Africa had made 19 without loss meaning that the crowd had seen 522 runs scored for the loss of just two wickets. When play resumed on 1 July England bowled out the Springboks for 240 to complete a victory by an innings and 18 runs, the exact margin that England had been victorious by in the first Test of the series at Edgbaston. To add to the oddities in the match South Africa's Tail End Charlie George Parker played his second and final Test for the Springboks, and is the only South African Test cricketer never to have played first class cricket in South Africa. Born in Cape Town, he was playing in the Bradford League when a South African team short of bowlers called him into the Test side for the first Test and for only his second first class match. In that game he took 6 for 152, including five wickets on the opening day and was so exhausted that he had to leave the field of play. After the second Test, he never played first class cricket again and eventually emigrated to Australia.

SATURDAY 30 JUNE 1973

Since the Minor Counties no longer play in cup competitions in England there is no real giant killing. That was not the case when Durham (then not playing first class cricket) beat Yorkshire in the Gillette Cup. Yorkshire captain Geoffrey Boycott won the toss and decided to bat. He saw his side tumble to 135 all out in 58.4 overs – Colin Johnson hit 44 before he hit his own wicket. Durham coasted to a five-wicket victory with almost ten overs to spare.

CRICKET
On This Day

JULY

SATURDAY 1 JULY 1916

Yorkshire all-rounder Major Booth killed in action aged 29 near La Cigny, France on the opening day of the Battle of the Somme. Despite his name Booth was actually a Second Lieutenant; he played twice for England on the 1913-14 tour of South Africa. His best bowling figures were 4 for 49 and he was *Wisden* Cricketer of the Year in 1914. His sister refused to believe that he had perished in the mud and lit a candle in his room which she kept untouched awaiting his return until her own death in 1950.

SATURDAY 1 JULY 2000

England beat West Indies by two wickets in the second Test at Lord's. England won the toss and decided to field. The match became a wicketfest with one falling every twenty-two deliveries and on the second day a part of all four innings occurred – the only such incident in Test history. The day began with the West Indies first innings at 267 for 9. West Indies then bowled England out for 134 before the home side had their revenge and dismissed the tourists for just 54. At close of play England in their second innings were 0 for 0. The home side made their target reaching 191 for the loss of eight wickets.

WEDNESDAY 2 JULY 1817

William Lambert became the first batsman to score a century in both innings in a match between Sussex and Epsom which began today at Lord's. Lambert scored 107 not out (of 292) in the first innings and first class career best 157 (of 445) in the second knock as Sussex won by 427 runs.

TUESDAY 2 JULY 1912

The greatest fast bowler of his generation Tom Richardson died of a heart attack on a walking holiday at St Jean d'Arvey, Chambery, Savoie in France. He was just 41 but his last years had been affected by his excessive drinking and a weight problem that ended his career in 1904. He made one appearance for Somerset in 1905 but the fire in his belly, that had seen him take 88 wickets in just 14 Tests with an innings best of 8 for 94 and a match best of 13 for 244, had gone. In all first class cricket he took more than 2,100 wickets. *Wisden* described his best years as being between 1893 and 1897 and commented, "It is quite safe to say that his work during those five years has never been surpassed" before adding the caveat, "Too much was exacted from him, but he ought not to have gone off as soon as he did. He began to lose efficiency before he was 28."

THURSDAY 3 JULY 1902

Bramall Lane, Sheffield staged its first – and indeed only – Test match when Australia beat England by 143 runs. The first day's play ended early because of bad light and the second day's was interrupted by rain. The ground was first used in 1855 but has primarily been a venue for football and is home to Sheffield United. Financial woes led to Yorkshire playing their final game there in 1973 drawing with Lancashire in a match that ended on 7 August. That winter the Blades built a new stand on the open side of the ground and cricket was no more at Bramall Lane until July 2007 when Yorkshire Second XI played a match there.

TUESDAY 4 JULY 1837

The Players beat the Gentlemen in the "Barn Door Match". Games of cricket are often one-sided affairs but usually both sides start off with an equal chance. In this game that was not the case – the Players defended a wicket of four stumps measuring 36 inches by 12 inches while the Gentlemen defended three stumps of normal size (27 inches by eight inches). The Gentlemen batted first and were all out for 54 with William Lillywhite capturing nine wickets. The Players then made 99 with Ned Wenman scoring 35 and slow bowler James Cobbett an undefeated 32. No one else made double figures. Fuller Pilch was out after his hat fell on the wicket from a delivery by Sir Frederick Bathurst. The Gentlemen were then dismissed for 35 although the innings only featured two ducks. Scheduled for three days, the Players won by an innings and 10 runs inside two.

FRIDAY 4 JULY 1845

The wandering cricket club I Zingari ("the gypsies") was founded by Old Harrovians John Loraine Baldwin, Hon. Frederick Ponsonby (later 6th Earl of Bessborough), Hon. Spencer Ponsonby (later Sir Spencer Ponsonby-Fane) and Richard Penruddocke Long, during dinner at the Blenheim Hotel, Bond Street, London following a match against Harrow. One of the oldest cricket clubs and one of the few with no home ground, the only prime minister to play first class cricket Lord Home was governor (or leader) of the club from 1977 to 1989. Its matches were recorded in *Wisden Cricketers' Almanack* from 1867 until 2004. Barrister William Boland was named club president in perpetuity on 5 July 1845 and remains so long after his death.

SATURDAY 5 JULY 1958

Play finally got underway in the third Test between England and New Zealand after there was no play in the first two days. New Zealand won the toss and decided to bat. Five wickets from Jim Laker helped England bowl out the Kiwis for 67 with only the two openers Lawrie Miller (26) and John D'Arcy (11) making it to double figures. England declared on 267 for 2 with centuries from debutant Arthur Milton and captain Peter May. The England innings was opened by two players who had also represented their country in other sports: Mike Smith who made 3 had played rugby union in 1956 and Milton had played football in 1951 while on Arsenal's books. The Kiwis made 129 in their second innings and England won by an innings and 71 runs.

THURSDAY 5 JULY 1973

Former cricketer Dickie Bird umpired in his first Test match – the third England v New Zealand match at Headingley, Leeds.

TUESDAY 6 JULY 1993

Graham Thorpe became the fourteenth English batsman to score a century on his Test debut when hit 114 not out in the second innings of the third Ashes Test at Trent Bridge, Nottingham. He hit just six in the first innings in the match, which ended in a draw.

MONDAY 7 JULY 1806

The first Gentlemen v Players was played at Lord's Old Ground, Marylebone, Middlesex. Very little detail of the first match remains. The Players batted first and were all out for 69. Oddly, we know of only two bowlers who took wickets but we know who caught or in one case stumped the batsmen. The Gentlemen made 195 and again catchers and the wicketkeeper is known but only one bowler. The Players were all out in their second innings for 112. The only wicket for which we have complete details was taken (bowled) by Lord Frederick Beauclerk, the son of the 5th Duke of St Albans. The Gentlemen won by an innings and 14 runs. The ground was used from 1787 until 1810 when the ground was built upon after the lease ran out.

THURSDAY 7 JULY 2005

So-called "supersubs" used in a one day international for the first time when England played Australia at Headingley. The supersub could bat, bowl, field or keep wicket and as with football the substituted player took no further part in the game. The first supersub was Vikram Solanki who replaced Simon Jones after 31 overs of Australia's innings. Australia made 219 for 7 from their 50 overs. When England batted Brad Hogg replaced Matthew Hayden after 22 overs. England reached their total in just 46 overs making 221 with the loss of just Andrew Strauss and won by 9 wickets. It quickly became apparent that the supersub benefited the team that won the toss and the captains agreed not to use them by late 2005. On 15 February 2006, the ICC announced their intention to discontinue the supersub experiment.

MONDAY 8 JULY 1974

With an hour and six minutes to play on the second day of the 130th match between Cambridge University and Oxford University Edward Jackson, a 19 year old law student came into bat. He was 0 not out when stumps were drawn. The next day he batted for fifteen minutes before hitting a four to get off the mark. Roland Paver caught him the very next over. Although he never went on to a career in cricket, Jackson had the distinction of future Pakistan Test captain Imran Khan claiming his wicket in both innings.

WEDNESDAY 8 JULY 2009

Sophia Gardens, Cardiff, home of Glamorgan, hosted a Test match for the first time as England played Australia in the opening game of the Ashes.

MONDAY 9 JULY 1893

Defensive batman Bill Scotton committed suicide aged 37 at his lodgings at 91 St John's Wood Road, London. He had suffered from depression for some time over losing his place in the Nottinghamshire county side. In the third Test against Australia on 12 August 1886 Scotton played for 225 minutes and only scored 34. It prompted *Punch* to write a parody of Alfred, Lord Tennyson:

> "Block, block, block
> At the foot of thy wicket, O Scotton!
> And I would that my tongue would utter
> My boredom. You won't put the pot on!
> Block, block, block,
> At the foot of thy wicket, ah do!
> But one hour of Grace or Walter Read
> Were worth a week of you!"

WEDNESDAY 10 JULY 1974

Brian Luckhurst of Kent became the first player to score 1,000 runs in Gillette Cup matches – the milestone coming in his 24th match (against Durham at Canterbury).

THURSDAY 10 JULY 1975

Future Essex and England captain Graham Gooch made his Test debut against Australia at Edgbaston. Unfortunately, Gooch scored a pair spending just eight minutes in the middle and facing ten balls. He was the first batsman since Fred Grace in September 1880 to get a pair on his debut. England didn't fare any better – Australia won the match by an innings and 85 runs. Gooch played one more Test making 6 and 31 before he was dropped from the side and went back to Essex where he reinvented himself as an opening batsman, returning to the Test arena in the summer of 1978 against Pakistan.

FRIDAY 11 JULY 1884

Test cricket started at Old Trafford – a day late because of the rain. The Australians had arrived to play a series of three matches against England – the first rubber of more than one match to be played on English soil. The first Test was scheduled to begin on 10 July 1884 but thanks to Manchester's rainy weather the first day was a complete washout.

FRIDAY 11 JULY 1930

Don Bradman scored the fastest double century in a Test match when he scored 200 for Australia against England at Headingley in just 214 minutes. Batting today and tomorrow he made 334 – then the highest individual score in Test cricket – out of a total of 566. Bradman passed 5,500 runs in first class matches when he reached 117. The match ended in a draw.

TUESDAY 12 JULY 1932

Yorkshire beat Nottinghamshire by 10 wickets – thanks in no small part to their bowler Hedley Verity who claimed all 10 Nottinghamshire second innings wickets at a cost of just 10 runs. In the first innings he took 2 for 64 but when Nottinghamshire came out for their second knock Verity took them apart and returned figures of 19.4 overs of which 16 were maidens, 10 wickets for 10 runs. Of the victims eight were caught, one was stumped and one was lbw but none were clean bowled.

WEDNESDAY 12 JULY 1950

A County Championship match at Old Trafford ended in one day for the first time since 1925. Lancashire met Sussex on a pitch that the visitors' captain, James Langridge, said was not fit for a three-day match. Thirty wickets fell for 391 runs and the captains agreed to extra time to finish the match. Sussex batted first after winning the toss and were bowled out for 101 with spinner Malcolm Hilton taking 6 for 32. Lancashire responded with 239 and Geoff Edrich, brother of Bill, hitting 89 and Jack Oakes taking 5 for 107. Sussex were then bowled out for 51 with Hilton taking 5 for 18 and Peter Greenwood 5 for 24 as Lancashire won by an innings and 87 runs.

MONDAY 13 JULY 1840

The ball vanished at Lord's Cricket Ground, St John's Wood during a match between MCC and North. MCC batted first and were all out for 71 and the North did not fare much better making just 81. However, at one stage Samuel Dakin and debutant Abraham Bass (making a career best 10 before being run out) were at the crease when a stroke was hit to the outfield where it was collected by Old Etonian George Liddell who flung it back to the wicket with great force. It hit Bass's hat, knocked it off and disappeared. A new ball was used for the rest of the innings and some time later the ball was discovered stuck between the crown and lining.

SATURDAY 13 JULY 2002

India beat England in the NatWest Series Final at Lord's by two wickets with just three balls remaining. England batted first and made 325 for 5 with centuries from Marcus Trescothick (109) and captain Nasser Hussain (115). At one stage India were 146 for 5 and batsmen Sourav Ganguly, Sachin Tendulkar and Rahul Dravid were all out. It came down to Mohammad Kaif and Yuvraj Singh who added 121 in 106 balls before Kaif hit the winning run off Freddie Flintoff.

MONDAY 14 JULY 1890

John Rawlin became the first man to play and umpire in the County Championship. Unusually, he umpired first and made his playing debut today for Middlesex against Surrey at Lord's.

SATURDAY 14 JULY 1984

Fast bowler Malcolm Marshall batted one handed and scored 4 runs as West Indies beat England at Headingley by 8 wickets to win the third Test. Marshall had doubly fractured his left thumb while fielding but took to the field letting Larry Gomes remain undefeated on 104.

MONDAY 15 JULY 1822

John Willes of Kent became the first bowler to be no-balled for throwing. He had been practising with his sister Christine and because of her voluminous skirts, she could only bowl round armed. Willes found it difficult to play and so adopted the style when he played for Kent against MCC at Lord's. He left the ground in "high dudgeon" when the umpire ruled against him and refused to play, leaving another player to replace him. It would not be until 1828 that MCC authorised round-arm bowling.

MONDAY 15 JULY 1996

The libel case between Ian Botham and Allan Lamb versus Imran Khan opened with George Carman, QC representing the Pakistani former captain and Charles Grey, QC the two English Test players before Mr Justice French. Botham and Lamb had accused Imran Khan of calling them cheats and racists who lacked class, allegations he denied. Among the star witnesses were Mike Atherton (taking a break from a Test match, ironically against Pakistan), Derek Pringle, David Lloyd, David Gower, John Emburey, Brian Close and Geoff Boycott. Disinterested observers believed that Botham and Lamb would win the case and were "astonished" when the jury found by a majority for Imran. An appeal was abandoned in May 1999.

THURSDAY 16 JULY 1868

Surrey played Lancashire at The Oval in the County Championship and owing to the intense heat the match was suspended for an hour.

MONDAY 16 JULY 1984

Bodyline came to Australian television. It was the name of a seven-part mini-series dramatising the events of the 1932-33 Test rubber. It starred Gary Sweet as Don Bradman, Hugo Weaving as Douglas Jardine, John Doyle as Gubby Allen, Jim Holt as Harold Larwood, Rhys McConnochie as Pelham Warner and John Walton as Bert Woodfull. The programme was released with the tagline "The day England declared war on Australia".

TUESDAY 17 JULY 1888

The crowd at Lord's saw 27 wickets fall in a single day in the first Test between England and Australia. A heavy overnight downpour hit Middlesex which left the pitch a sea of mud and also meant that the game could not start till 3pm. Resuming at 18 for 3 with W. G. Grace not out on 10, Australia bowled out England for 53 in less than an hour. Australia were then dismissed for 60 before England were again bowled out for 62 at 4.25pm. In a day 27 wickets fell for 157 runs in slightly more than three hours of play.

SATURDAY 17 JULY 2004

Warwickshire's Nick Knight had the misfortune to be run out twice in the same innings. Playing in the Cheltenham & Gloucester Trophy semi-final against Worcestershire he was run out for 37 as Warwickshire chased a total of 257 for 4 off fifty overs. His dismissal left them at 93 for 3. Later in the innings Knight returned to the fray as a runner for Ian Trott but found himself once again run out. Worse still, Warwickshire lost by 41 runs.

TUESDAY 18 JULY 1848

The Grand Old Man of Cricket W.G. Grace born at Downend, Bristol and began playing first-class cricket when he was fifteen. He combined his sporting prowess with his studying to become a doctor. In a playing career that lasted thirty-seven years he hit 54,211 runs including 124 centuries and on ten separate occasions scored more than 200 runs. He took 876 catches and made five stumpings, he took 2,809 wickets and in 1879 he announced his partial retirement to concentrate on his medical practice: "I have bowled many a maiden over in my time but to make up for that I hope to set many a one on her legs again."

THURSDAY 18 JULY 1907

Surrey's wicketkeeping bad boy Ted Pooley died broken and bankrupt in Lambeth Infirmary, aged 65. His career was bighted by his perhaps understandable desire to make money. In 1873 Surrey suspended him after he had a bet on a game for a bottle of champagne and when he won, he drank his winnings for breakfast with the result that by lunchtime he was in no fit state to play and was replaced behind the stumps (see 6 April 1877).

THURSDAY 19 JULY 1877

Spencer Gore won the first Wimbledon Gentlemen's Singles final using laws drawn up by MCC. He was captain of Harrow XI and made two appearances for Surrey as well as first-class outings for I Zingari and Gentlemen of the South but it was in tennis that he found his metier. He played four matches without dropping a set and won the final 6-1, 6-2, 6-4 against William Marshall in front of 200 spectators. He received 12 guineas and a silver cup. The final was actually delayed for three days by rain and two more when the spectators went off to watch the obviously more important Eton-Harrow match at Lord's.

SATURDAY 19 JULY 1952

India became the only Test side to be dismissed twice in the same day. In the third Test against England at Old Trafford, the home team declared at 347 for 9 with Len Hutton, England's first professional captain, scoring 104. England's Freddie Trueman then bowled out India for 58 with only two players making double figures – Trueman's figures were 8 for 31. India went into bat again and this time made 82 with Alec Bedser and Tony Lock taking nine wickets between them and Trueman only taking one thus failing to get 10 wickets in a match. England won the match by an innings and 207 runs.

THURSDAY 20 JULY 1899

Hampshire began their innings against Somerset in the County Championship at County Ground, Taunton having bowled out the home team for 315. When Hampshire crashed to 65 for 4 by close of play today it seemed as if Somerset would have an easy victory. However, the next day Robert Poore hit a career best 304, Tom Poore hit a career best 95 and captain Teddy Wynyard weighed in with 225 to finish the day on 672 for 7 declared. Poore and Wynyard put on 411 for the sixth wicket in four hours and twenty minutes. Poore batted for 410 minutes and hit 45 fours in his innings of 304. What was remarkable was that Somerset did not concede one bye in the entire innings. What was even more remarkable was that their wicketkeeper was a 43-year-old clergyman the Reverend Prebendary Archie Wickham. Even with divine assistance, he could not prevent Hampshire winning by an innings and 151 runs.

MONDAY 20 JULY 1908

Middlesex beat Gentlemen of Philadelphia at Lord's by seven wickets in a three-day match that was over in just one. In their first innings Gentlemen of Philadelphia were bowled out for 58 with Frank Tarrant taking 5 for 19 and Albert Trott 5 for 31. Middlesex made 92 (and Tarrant opened the innings becoming second top scorer) before dismissing Gentlemen of Philadelphia for 55 with Tarrant picking up another five wickets (for 27) and Trott 4 for 28. Trott opened the second knock for Middlesex and made 10 before they achieved their winning target – 24 for 3.

MONDAY 21 JULY 1884

Lord's staged its first Test match when England played Australia in the second Test – and won by an innings and five runs. It was also the first Test in which a substitute fielder took a catch – Australian captain Billy Murdoch having batted and fielding for England (because W.G. Grace had hurt his finger) caught fellow countryman Tup Scott.

TUESDAY 21 JULY 1981

Already one down in the series England came from behind at Headingley to become only the second time in Test history that a side following on had won the match. Australia won the toss, decided to bat and cleared at 401 for 9, John Dyson top scoring with 102, his maiden Test century. Ian Botham took 6 for 95. England were then dismissed for 174, a plucky 50 from Botham being the top score. With a deficit of 227, England were ordered to follow on. At one stage they were 41 for 4 (Graham Gooch, captain Mike Brearley, David Gower and Mike Gatting all surrendering their wickets cheaply). Opener Geoff Boycott hung around for 46 but it was Botham and Graham Dilley who came to England's rescue. Dilley hit a career best 56 but it was Botham who using one of Gooch's bats hit an undefeated 149 in 148 balls and 219 minutes including 27 fours and one six. The England players had already booked out of the hotel so confident were they of defeat and had to rebook for the Monday night. Australia needed 130 to win and were still odds on favourites. At 56 for 1 that victory seemed assured. Then the collapse began – Trevor Chappell became the first of Bob Willis's eight victims that day as the tall fast bowler took a career best 8 for 43. Australia were 111 all out and England won by 18 runs.

FRIDAY 22 JULY 1887

W.G. Grace saved a teammate's life. Gloucestershire were playing Lancashire at Old Trafford Cricket Ground, Stretford, Manchester when attempting to prevent a four Arthur Croome slipped and impaled his throat on the spiked railings. Team captain Grace held the wound together for more than half an hour until help could arrive. Had the doctor not been there and known what to do Croome would have undoubtedly bled to death.

SATURDAY 22 JULY 1916

Fast bowler Percy Jeeves killed aged 28 at High Wood, Montauban, France during the Battle of the Somme while serving with the Royal Warwickshire Regiment. Four years earlier, he had played for Warwickshire against the Australians and South Africans even though he had not lived long enough in the county to be qualified. He finally qualified in 1913 and took 106 wickets and scored 765 runs in first-class matches that season. In 1914 he took 90 wickets and Plum Warner predicted that Jeeves would soon be selected for England. A month later, the First World War began. Jeeves played his last first class match at Edgbaston against Surrey and took 5 for 52 and 2 for 36. In 1913 one of the spectators who watched Jeeves play was the novelist P.G. Wodehouse and in 1915 he created the character of Bertie Wooster and appropriated the name of Percy Jeeves for Wooster's valet (albeit changing his Christian name to Reginald).

WEDNESDAY 23 JULY 1879

Experience saw off youth at Lord's as a team of over 30s beat a team of under 30s in a match played for the benefit of W.G. Grace who received a marble clock and some money in front of the pavilion on the second day. Under 30 won the toss and decided to bat. Thanks to inclement weather the first day was lost and the second day's play did not begin until 1.15pm. The Under 30s were bowled out for 111 with Fred Grace the top scorer on 35 not out. Big brother W.G. took 3 for 54. Over 30 scored 138 in their first innings although W.G. was out for a duck. Frank Townsend scored 43 and Edward Grace, the third member of the family to play, contributed 40. Future England bowler Dick Barlow took 5 for 32. Under 30 scored 80 in their second knock and W.G. took 6 for 33. The Over 30s made their target at 5.25pm reaching 54 for 3 to win by seven wickets.

THURSDAY 23 JULY 1942

Surrey Test batsman Andrew Ducat died of a heart attack while batting for Surrey Home Guard against Sussex Home Guard at Lord's. A former Arsenal midfielder, he was one of the few people to have represented England at international level at both football and cricket. He was 56 and is the only person in history to have died during a match at Lord's.

TUESDAY 24 JULY 1821

The Players beat the Gentlemen in the Coronation Match to commemorate the crowning of King George IV. The Gentlemen batted first but were bowled out for just 60. The Players were on 278 for 6 when the Gentlemen conceded the match. It marked the last appearance of "Silver Billy" Beldham who was reputed to have fathered 39 children.

SATURDAY 24 JULY 1954

Pakistan middle-order batsman Ebbu Ghazli got a pair in just two hours at Old Trafford, Manchester, during the third Test against England. At 4.14pm he went into bat and was caught by David Sheppard off the bowling of Johnny Wardle. Exactly two hours later, Wardle caught him off Alec Bedser's delivery.

FRIDAY 25 JULY 1884

The County Championship match between Lancashire and Gloucestershire at Old Trafford, Manchester was abandoned following the death of Martha Grace, the mother of W.G. and E.M. – the only such occurrence of a game being stopped over a death of a non-player.

FRIDAY 25 JULY 1986

England wicketkeeper Bruce French was injured when hit on the head by a Richard Hadlee delivery while batting and retired hurt on 0 at Lord's in the first Test against New Zealand. When it was New Zealand's turn to bat England used four players behind the stumps: Bill Athey took the gloves for the first two overs before veteran Bob Taylor who had retired two years earlier took over for overs three to seventy-six. Taylor had been at the match to enjoy the hospitality and had to wear borrowed kit although perhaps presciently he did have his own gloves in the boot of his car. Hampshire keeper Bobby Parks was there for overs seventy-seven to one hundred and forty before French returned for the final ball.

SATURDAY 26 JULY 1902

Australia beat England by the second smallest margin in Ashes Tests – just three runs – at Old Trafford. Australia won the toss, decided to bat and were all out for 299 with 104 of those runs coming from Victor Trumper and 65 from Clem Hill. Fast bowler Bill Lockwood took 6 for 48. England made 262 and medium fast bowler Stanley Jackson was the highest scorer with 128. Lockwood took 5 for 28 in Australia's second innings as they collapsed to 86 all out. With only a small target to reach, England were dismissed for 120 with Hugh Trumble taking 6 for 53.

SATURDAY 26 JULY 1924

Having already won the series against South Africa, England gathered at Old Trafford hoping to make it four victories in a row. The Springboks won the toss and elected to bat before 8,000 spectators. Torrential rain ended the day's play at 4pm after 165 minutes during which time South Africa made 116 for 4. Rain prevented play on the rest of the scheduled days and opener Jack MacBryan's Test career began and ended. Slated to bat at number three, he is the only Test cricketer never to bat, bowl or field.

TUESDAY 27 JULY 1948

Australia won the fourth Test against England by 7 wickets – the first time that a side batting fourth had won after needing more than 400 runs for victory. It was the third win in the series for Australia. England won the toss and elected to bat. They made 496 with centuries from Cyril Washbrook (143) and Bill Edrich (111). Australia made 458 with Neil Harvey top scoring with 112. Norman Yardley declared the England innings closed at 365 for 8 leaving Australia 404 to win. Thanks to 182 from Arthur Morris and an unbeaten 173 from Don Bradman Australia won with ease.

THURSDAY 27 JULY 2006

Ashwell Prince became the first black captain of South Africa when he led the team at the Sinhalese Sports Club Ground, Colombo, in the first match against Sri Lanka following the unavailability of Graeme Smith and Jacques Kallis. Prince won the toss and elected to bat but the Sri Lankans dumped the Springboks out for 169 with Prince contributing just 1. Sri Lanka began unimpressively and were 14 for 2 until captain Mahela Jayawardene and Kumar Sangakkara came to the wicket. They shared a world record partnership of 624 before the third wicket fell. Jayawardene scored 374 and

Sangakkara was not far behind on 287. South Africa responded with a respectable 434 but not one player reached triple figures and Sri Lanka won by an innings and 153 runs.

WEDNESDAY 28 JULY 1971

Lancashire met Gloucestershire in the semi-final of the Gillette Cup at Old Trafford, Manchester, before 23,520 spectators. Holders Lancashire won the toss and decided to field. Gloucestershire scored 229 for the loss of six wickets in their sixty overs. Opener Ron Nicholls scored 53; Mike Procter was the top scorer with 65. The match continued but more than an hour's play was lost after lunch to rain. David Lloyd and Barry Wood made 61 for Lancashire's first wicket and 105 was on the board by the time the second wicket fell. At 7.30pm umpires Dickie Bird and Arthur Jepson decided that they wanted the match to be concluded that night. As the light faded Gloucestershire took more and more time to bowl their overs and slowly they whittled away at the Lancashire batsmen. Clive Lloyd went for 34 and India's Test wicketkeeper Farokh Engineer was out when he slipped and touched the wicket with his foot when he had only two to his name. His was the sixth wicket to fall with the score on 163 which left Lancashire 67 to score at a run rate of almost five and in increasingly poor light. Captain Jack Bond batted solidly allowing off-break bowler Jack Simmons to wallop his fellow off-breaker John Mortimore when he could actually see the ball. Eventually, Mortimore bowled Simmons for 25. At about 8.45pm David Hughes went out to bat. The story goes that 24-year-old Hughes spent time in a darkened dressing room to get his eyes adjusted to the poor light before he went out to the crease. Hughes faced Mortimore at the start of the 56th over with 25 needed from five overs. Hughes made himself a hero as he hit Mortimore for 6, 4, 2, 2, 4 and 6 to total 24 runs and ensure certain victory for the northerners. Bond scored the winning run off Proctor in the next over.

SATURDAY 29 JULY 1944

The Germans "invaded" Lord's during a match between the Army and Royal Air Force. As Jack Robertson batted, a Doodlebug was heard approaching and both players and spectators took "evasive action" by lying flat on the ground. When the flying bomb was safely out of harm's way (as far as the cricket was concerned) Robertson responded, hitting Bob Wyatt for a six.

THURSDAY 29 JULY 2004

Pakistan fast bowler Mohammad Sami earned the dubious honour of bowling the longest over in One Day Internationals. Playing against Bangladesh in the Second Phase of the Asia Cup at R. Premadasa Stadium, Colombo Sami opened the bowling with Shabbir Ahmed and after a maiden he delivered a 17-ball over, which included seven wides and four no-balls for 22 runs in all. In spite of his erratic bowling Pakistan won by 6 wickets.

SATURDAY 30 JULY 1904

Sir Herbert Jenner-Fust died aged 98 at Hill Court, Falfield, Gloucestershire. An Old Etonian and president of MCC he was the last survivor of the first Oxford-Cambridge match in 1827 – he scored 47 out of Cambridge's 92 in the rain-ruined game. Jenner as he was known in his playing days was an opening batsman, wicketkeeper ("pads were not heard of in my days and the player would be laughed at who attempted to protect his shins") and semi underarm bowler and was described by Lord Harris as "the first gentleman player in the country". Jenner retired from competitive cricket to practise law. Despite his son playing alongside him, Jenner "never took the trouble to see W.G. Grace play". Jenner's son, also Herbert, died on 11 November 1940, aged 99 – they spanned an era of 134 years, 8 months and 20 days – one month after the death of William Pitt the Younger to the Battle of Britain.

THURSDAY 30 JULY 1914

One of the few men to play Test cricket for England and Australia Albert Edwin Trott shot himself aged 41 at his lodgings at Denbigh Road, Willesden Green, Middlesex. He had been suffering from dropsy and depression and wrote his will on the back of a laundry ticket, leaving his clothes and £4 to his landlady. In his day "Albatrott" had been one of the best all-rounders in England and was *Wisden* Cricketer of the Year in 1899. He played three Tests for Australia – all against England in 1894-1895 – and then played twice for England against South Africa in 1899.

MONDAY 31 JULY 1899

Australian Albert Trott playing for MCC against the touring Australians became the only batsman to hit a ball over the current Lord's pavilion, smashing Monty Noble out of the ground on his way to 41. Despite his best efforts – he also took three wickets – the Australians won by nine wickets.

CRICKET
On This Day

AUGUST

WEDNESDAY 1 AUGUST 1866

Having spent the two preceding days at The Oval scoring 224 not out for England against Surrey, W.G. Grace won the 440 yards hurdles at the first meeting of the National Olympian Association at Crystal Palace.

MONDAY 1 AUGUST 1988

In a bid to force a result between Dorset and Cheshire in a Minor Counties match at Sherborne School Dorset skipper Reverend Andrew Wingfield Digby ordered bowler Graeme Calway to bowl wides and set the field including the wicketkeeper so that the ball could reach the boundary. As a result Calway bowled fourteen wides and was hit for a four meaning that his over cost 60 runs. The reverend's actions meant that Cheshire needed 53 to win in ten overs and Dorset needed four wickets. The home side prevailed and Dorset won by 18 runs but of 182 runs scored by Cheshire in their second innings 69 came in Extras including 60 from just one over.

FRIDAY 2 AUGUST 1805

Lord Byron played cricket for Harrow against Eton in the annual match at Lord's Old Ground, Dorset Square, London despite being handicapped with a clubfoot. With the help of a runner, Byron made seven in Harrow's first innings, out of a total score of 55. Eton made 122 in their innings and Byron took one wicket bowling John Kaye for seven. Harrow were dismissed for 65 in their second innings and Byron made just two. Eton College won by an innings and 2 runs. In both innings Byron followed into bat a pupil called Shakespear.

TUESDAY 2 AUGUST 1977

At 4.42pm England beat Australia in a Test at Trent Bridge for the first time since 1930 to go 2-0 up in the rubber. A 21-year-old Somerset all-rounder by the name of Ian Botham had made his Test debut and taken 5 for 74 in Australia's first innings. Making a return to the international arena after a self-imposed absence of 30 Tests was Geoff Boycott who celebrated with his thirteenth Test ton and 98th in all first-class cricket. He was undefeated on 80 in England's second innings. Alan Knott scored 135 to become the first wicketkeeper to score 4,000 runs in Test cricket and play was held up for eight minutes on the first day (28 July) so that the teams could be presented to H.M. the Queen and H.R.H. the Duke of Edinburgh during her Silver Jubilee celebrations.

MONDAY 3 AUGUST 1874

A touring team made up of twenty-two American baseball players (eleven from Boston and eleven from Philadelphia) began their first match in England against the Gentlemen of MCC. Their tour was designed "to give the English a practical insight into the workings of base ball". They played five matches in England and one in Dublin winning three and drawing three including the match that began today against MCC. The 12 of MCC scored 105 runs but the 18 of America scored two more.

THURSDAY 3 AUGUST 1978

Benjamin Huntsman Williams became the first first class cricketer to be murdered during the conflict in Rhodesia. Rocket-wielding terrorists attacked his car. He made his first-class debut in 1966-1967 and was a regular member of the Rhodesian team in 1969-1970.

WEDNESDAY 4 AUGUST 1886

Andrew Stoddart scored a then world record 485 – including one eight, three fives, and 64 fours – in 370 minutes for Hampstead against Stoics. In the days before cricketers spent hours practising in the nets and eating healthy foods, Stoddart was up all night before the match playing poker and after he was out he went off to play tennis and then went out for dinner in the evening.

MONDAY 4 AUGUST 1975

Merchant navy cook Michael Angelow stripped down to his trainers and socks and ran on to the pitch at Lord's and hurdled both sets of stumps to become the first streaker at a Test match. Sixteen months earlier Australian stockbroker Michael O'Brien bet a friend that streaking would catch on in Britain. He then ran onto the pitch during a rugby union international at Twickenham before famously being led away with only a policeman's helmet to preserve his modesty. (PC Bruce Perry later said: "I felt embarrassed so I covered him up as best I could. It was a cold day – he had nothing to be proud of.") O'Brien was fined by the courts and sacked by his employer, but at least he won his bet: by the end of the decade streaking had spread to several other sports, including cricket. When Angelow introduced streaking to cricket during the second Test of the 1975 Ashes series reactions were mixed: Greg Chappell was not amused; Alan Turner is said to have roared with laughter, and one commentator simply said: "Well I've seen nothing like this at Lord's before." The crowd cheered, and journalists had a field day with puns about no-balls, googlies, ball tampering and merchant seamen. Even the St John's Wood magistrates saw the funny side, fining Angelow the exact amount that he had won in a bet with his friends (various reports put the size of the bet and the fine at £10, £20 and £25). More than twenty years later Greg Chappell was still not amused, grumpily complaining that Angelow had started a fad that demeaned the sport. Angelow, on the other hand, said that he loved cricket and had waited until the end of Dennis Lillee's over so as not to disrupt the game.

TUESDAY 5 AUGUST 1794

Westminster (171) beat Charterhouse (42 and 24) by an innings and 105 runs in the first known inter-school match at Dorset Square, Lord's for a purse of 500 guineas.

SATURDAY 5 AUGUST 2006

Ireland debutant Eoin Morgan let his enthusiasm get the better of him against Scotland in a one day international at Cambusdoon New Ground, Ayr. He became the first batsman to be run out for 99 on his debut and swore loudly as he left the crease. Officials reprimanded him but three years later their troubles were ended when Morgan was chosen for the England one-day squad.

FRIDAY 6 AUGUST 1943

Tom Garrett died at Warrawee, Sydney, aged 85 years 11 days. He was the last surviving player from the first Test match in March 1877. An all-rounder, he played 19 Tests scoring 339 runs with a top score of 51 not out. He took 36 wickets with an innings best of 6 for 78 and a match best of 9 for 163.

SATURDAY 6 AUGUST 2005

Craig Perkins, a 30-year-old quantity surveyor, and his friend Andrew Jones who were dressed as bunny girls refused admission to Edgbaston for the second Ashes Test after a stewardess with no sense of humour said that the outfits offended her. "We spent nearly £50 on those outfits," moaned Mr Perkins. "Dressing up is all part of the fun of going down to the cricket, especially on the Saturday." Luckily, the two men had a change of clothes with them – and England won the match by two runs.

THURSDAY 7 AUGUST 1997

The Hollioake brothers – Ben and Adam – make their Test debuts together for England against Australia at Trent Bridge to become the fifth set of brothers to represent a country in the international arena.

SUNDAY 7 AUGUST 2005

England beat Australia by just two runs in the second Ashes Test, at Edgbaston, to level the series. Ricky Ponting of Australia won the toss and, despite losing his main bowler, Glenn McGrath, when he stood on a cricket ball and tore his ankle ligaments before the match put England in to bat with the result that England made 407. Marcus Trescothick scored 90 and was top scorer. Australia in their first knock were all out for 308 before England collapsed to 182 in their second innings. Set a target of 282 Freddie Flintoff took four wickets to ensure that the Aussies fell short of their target and wrapped up the game in four days.

WEDNESDAY 8 AUGUST 1888

The first Ireland v Scotland match played at Observatory Lane, Rathmines, Dublin. Scotland won the toss and decided to bat. They were bowled out for 65 and 21-year-old Archibald Penny took 6 for 22. Ireland made 142 in their first innings but no batsman made more than 37 (scored by two players the captain and the wicketkeeper). English-born fast bowler George Robinson took 5 for 58. Scotland then made 51 with Westminster-born Charles Leggatt the top scorer on 13 not out as Ireland won by an innings and 26 runs.

WEDNESDAY 8 AUGUST 1956

Gloucestershire achieved the lowest first class total to include a double century against Glamorgan at Newport when they were all out for 298 – 200 undefeated runs were scored by Tom Graveney who began batting when the score was 9 for 2. He hit his double ton in 340 minutes and included three sixes and twenty fours. He also had the satisfaction of knowing that his team won the match.

FRIDAY 9 AUGUST 1991

Ian Botham's dismissal, courtesy of Curtly Ambrose in The Oval Test match resulted in the greatest sporting commentary of all time according to 78 per cent of Radio 5 Live listeners who voted in the poll. Botham had attempted to hook Ambrose and lost his balance dislodging the bail with his right thigh. Jonathan Agnew said, "He just didn't quite get his leg over." Fellow commentator Brian Johnston and Agnew dissolved into helpless giggles with Johnston begging, "Aggers, do stop it" as he tried to read the scorecard.

SUNDAY 9 AUGUST 1992

David Gower played in his last Test match – a 10-wicket defeat by Pakistan at The Oval. His final knock was a disappointing 1 before Waqar Younis bowled him. It was a sad end to a career that had its ups and downs (often off the pitch) over 117 Tests and 18 centuries with a top score of 215. Gower played a record 119 consecutive Test innings without a duck. He captained the England side on thirty-two occasions but won just five, drew nine and lost eighteen times.

MONDAY 10 AUGUST 1789

The first cricket tourists from England arrived in Dover ready for embarkation to Paris. John Frederick Sackville, 3rd Duke of Dorset was a devoted patron of cricket and responsible for a number of matches. In August 1789 he was the British ambassador in Paris and decided that it would be a good idea to further cement Anglo-French relations by arranging a goodwill cricket tour. He wrote to the Duke of Leeds, then Foreign Secretary and another cricketing enthusiast, to seek his assurances that the government would be supportive of the tour. Events overtook the tour and the team were met by the Duke of Dorset arriving post haste from Paris having fled the French Revolution.

SATURDAY 10 AUGUST 1991

Spinner Phil Tufnell's 6 for 25 at The Oval forced West Indies to follow on against England for the first time in 22 years and 48 Tests. It was Viv Richards' 50th and last Test as captain and Engand won by five wickets.

WEDNESDAY 11 AUGUST 1909

Warren Bardsley of Australia became the first cricketer to score a century in both innings of a Test match when he hit 130 in the second knock of the fifth Test at The Oval. Opening the batting, he had scored 136 in the first innings. Bardsley was one of Australia's greatest left-handed batsmen. He scored 29 centuries in England and by the time of his death in 1971 only Sir Donald Bradman and Lindsay Hassett had beaten his record of 53 centuries.

THURSDAY 11 AUGUST 1977

Geoff Boycott became the first player to score his 100th first-class century in a Test match when in his 645th innings he made his ton against Australia.

TUESDAY 12 AUGUST 1884

Wicketkeeper the Honourable Alfred Lyttelton took four wickets as England bowled out Australia for 551 with two players scoring a century and Billy Murdoch 211 – then the highest Test score. During Australia's innings, all eleven England players took a turn to bowl, the first time such an event occurred. Lyttelton bowled two spells and Walter Read and W.G. Grace kept wicket while he took his turn with the ball and amazingly turned out to be England's most successful bowler delivering a dozen overs, five maidens and taking 4 wickets for 19. He also wore his pads as he bowled. It was all rather in vain, however, as the match petered out into a draw.

MONDAY 12 AUGUST 1991

West Indies' greatest batsman Viv Richards played his 121st and last Test match. He was captain as West Indies lost by 5 wickets to an England side led by Graham Gooch. "Zap" won the toss and elected to bat with England making 419 (Robin Smith 109, Gooch 60, "Extras" 54) before bowling out the tourists for 176 (Phil Tufnell 6 for 25). Richards, batting unusually low down the order at number eight, scored just 2. Gooch enforced the follow-on and the West Indians made 385 (Richie Richardson 121, Richards 60, David "Syd" Lawrence 5 for 106). It was not a big enough target and England achieved it with the loss of Gooch, Hugh Morris, Michael Atherton, Robin Smith and Mark Ramprakash. The series ended in a two-all draw. Richards who had made his Test debut against India in 1974 retired from first-class cricket in 1993. He would have played more Tests had he not signed for Kerry Packer's World Series Cricket; he was knighted in 1999. In December 2002 *Wisden Cricketers' Almanack* chose him as the greatest one day international batsman of all time and third greatest ever Test batsman.

WEDNESDAY 13 AUGUST 1902

England batsman Gilbert Jessop played what many regard as the greatest innings of all time. Jessop was playing against Australia in the fifth Test at the Oval and England needed 263 to win on a pitch that favoured bowlers. That became apparent when England collapsed to 48 for 5. Then Jessop came to the crease and proceeded to smash the Aussie bowling around the field. He made 104 out of 139 in 75 minutes and England won the match by one wicket – the first time such a margin of victory occurred.

MONDAY 14 AUGUST 1933

England dismissed West Indies for 100 at The Oval – the first Test at the home ground of Surrey CCC and third of the series. England won by an innings and 17 runs.

SATURDAY 14 AUGUST 1948

Don Bradman played his last innings for Australia, against England at The Oval and received a standing ovation from the crowd and players as he made his way to the middle. He needed just four runs to retire with a Test batting average of 100. However, Eric Hollies had other ideas and bowled Bradman second ball for a duck. Bradman finished on an average of 99.94. Bradman claimed that he could not see properly because he had tears in his eyes although England wicketkeeper Godfrey Evans disputed that. And Hollies was most upset: "My best ball of the bloody season and they're clapping him!"

TUESDAY 15 AUGUST 1893

Leg-spinner Charles Townsend, 16, became the only bowler to achieve a hat-trick in which all victims were stumped. Playing for Gloucestershire alongside W.G. and E.M. Grace he took 4 for 16 but Somerset won by 127 runs.

MONDAY 15 AUGUST 1977

At 4.39pm England regained the Ashes when wicketkeeper Rodney Marsh skied a ball and fidgety fielder Derek Randall caught it off Mike Hendrick's delivery. England won by an innings and 85 runs. In their first innings they scored 436;opening batsman Geoff Boycott batted for 629 minutes and scored his 100th first-class century in his 645th innings. He was finally out, caught Greg Chappell bowled Len Pascoe for 191. He scored 48 per cent of England's total off the bat with wicketkeeper Alan Knott coming a distant second on 57. Australia were skittled out for just 103 with Rick McCosker top scoring on 27 and David Hookes not far behind on 24. Ian Botham took 5 wickets in an innings for a second consecutive match finishing on 5 for 21 and capturing the wickets of Hookes, Doug Walters, Marsh, Max Walker and Jeff Thomson. The Aussies made more of a fight in the second innings but were bowled out for 248 with Marsh putting up resistance before the superb catch from Randall ended Australia's hopes.

MONDAY 16 AUGUST 1813

James Bridger and his dog Drake beat J. Cock and W. Wetherell in a single wicket match at Holt Pound Cricket Ground, near Farnham in Surrey. After the first innings one man and his dog had scored 50 and the two men 6. Bridger scored all the fifty runs as Drake the dog neither batted not bowled and the two humans conceded defeat.

SUNDAY 16 AUGUST 1970

Kent's Bob Woolmer became the first bowler to take 50 wickets in the John Player League; a feat he achieved in his 26th match, which was against Gloucestershire at Chelmsford.

TUESDAY 17 AUGUST 1976

The Oval Test match between England and West Indies ended with a West Indian victory by 231 runs. This is the match in which commentator Brian Johnston did not say to BBC World Service listeners, "You join us with the news that England are 52 for 3. The bowler's Holding, the batsman's Willey." At no stage in the match were England ever at 52 for 3. In the first innings England had scored 151 by the loss of the third wicket and in the second inning they had already scored 54 when the second wicket went down. Another variant of the story comes from Henry Blofeld who recalls, "I suppose my classic memory was at the Oval in 1976 when England were doing better than usual – they were 81 for seven I think. Brian suddenly announced to an unsuspecting world: 'Well I can tell you the bowler's Holding the batsman's Willey'." Again, this is impossible – in the first innings England had scored 342 by the time the seventh wicket went down. In the second knock, the score was at 196 but Willey was fourth man out.

MONDAY 17 AUGUST 1981

England won the fifth Test against Australia and regained the Ashes – thanks to Ian Botham. England won the toss and decided to bat at Old Trafford, Manchester and Graham Gooch and Geoff Boycott began the England knock. Oddly, both were out for ten and England made 231 all out with Dennis Lillee and Terry Alderman equally sharing eight wickets between them. Botham scored a duck. Australia were dispatched for 130 with Bob Willis picking up four wickets and Botham three. In their second innings England collapsed to 104 for 5 when Botham strode in to join

Chris Tavaré at the crease. What followed was a tour de force as Botham struck 118 in 123 minutes off 102 balls including 66 off eight overs and six sixes. They added 149 for the sixth wicket – of which Tavaré added just 28. He was finally out after seven hours for 78 and took 304 minutes to reach his half-century. Thanks to Beefy, Tavaré and fifties from Alan Knott and John Emburey England made 404 all out. Terry Alderman was the top wicket taker with 5 for 109. Despite great performances from future captains Graham Yallop (114) and Allan Border (123 not out) Australia could only make 402 leaving England to win by 103 runs.

WEDNESDAY 18 AUGUST 1875

Somerset CCC founded by a team of amateurs at a meeting at Sidmouth, Devon. Somerset is still waiting to register its first County Championship.

SATURDAY 18 AUGUST 1951

Len Hutton became the first batsman to be dismissed obstructing the field in a Test match. England were chasing a target of 163 to beat South Africa at The Oval in the fifth Test and Hutton had scored 27 when he top edged a ball and to stop it from hitting the stumps he played at it a second time but in doing so he stopped debutant wicketkeeper Russell Endean from taking a catch. It didn't matter too much in the end – England won by four wickets (see 5 January 1957).

MONDAY 19 AUGUST 1816

A single wicket match at Sedley Green, Bexhill, Sussex became the first cricket match to be played under artificial light – thanks to candles in lanterns dotted around the pitch.

TUESDAY 19 AUGUST 1975

The third Test between England and Australia was abandoned after vandals wrecked the Headingley pitch with knives and oil protesting at the imprisonment of a man they claimed was innocent. Australia needed 225 runs to win the Test, go two up in the series and retain the Ashes with opening batsman Rick McCosker needing five more for his maiden Test century. Groundsman George Cawthray discovered the vandalism at the Rugby Ground End when he pushed back the covers. He could have repaired the holes in the pitch if they had not been filled with about a gallon of oil.

MONDAY 20 AUGUST 1900

Great Britain won the only Olympic Gold Medal for cricket when they beat France at the Exhibition Ground, Vincennes. Each side fielded twelve players and Great Britain batted first being all out for 117 with Frederick Cuming of MCC topping the scores with 38. Captain Charles Beachcroft was second with 23. For France W. Andersen took 4 wickets. In reply France were bowled out for 78 with Frederick W. Christian taking 7 Gallic wickets. In their second innings the British side scored 145 for 5 declared before dismissing the French for just 26 all out with only five minutes to spare before end of play. Montagu Toller took a remarkable 7 for 9. The Devon County Wanderers Club represented Britain while the French Athletic Club Union (which consisted almost entirely of Englishmen living in France and playing for the then Champions of France the Albion Cricket Club or for the Standard Athletic Club). Great Britain won by 158 runs.

SUNDAY 20 AUGUST 2006

After umpires Darrell Hair and Billy Doctrove accused them of ball tampering, Pakistan led by captain Inzamam-ul-Haq refused to retake the field in the The Oval Test. The umpires awarded England five penalty runs and the choice of a replacement ball, after ruling that Pakistan had illegally altered the ball. When the Pakistanis stayed in their dressing room, the umpires declared that the match could not be finished and left the field with the England team. The Pakistanis eventually returned to find an empty arena. Inzamam became the first captain in history to forfeit a Test match and was later charged with bringing the game into disrepute. On September 28, 2006 the allegations of ball tampering were dismissed but he was found guilty and suspended for four One Day Internationals. The ICC later changed the result and declared the match a draw.

TUESDAY 21 AUGUST 1866

Middlesex opener John Sewell became the first batsman to score a century in a pre-lunch session. He had begun the session on 29 not out and made 166 before he was out. It turned out to be his only first class ton.

THURSDAY 21 AUGUST 1952

Eccentric Australian batsman Sid Barnes sued in Sydney's District Court Jacob Raith, the writer of a letter to the Sydney afternoon paper *The Daily Mirror*, in which Mr Raith supported the decision by the Australian Board of Control to omit Barnes from the Test team "on grounds other than cricket ability". Jack Shand KC, Sydney's leading barrister, represented Barnes in the case and when he cross-examined the Board members it became apparent that they had listened to rumours about Barnes's reported bad behaviour – which was said to include insulting the Royal Family; stealing a car; drunkenness; jumping the turnstile at a ground when he forgot his player's pass and theft from teammates – without checking to see if the tales were true. The Board was also divided in its opinions of Barnes and he was vindicated with a full public apology.

TUESDAY 22 AUGUST 1939

England and West Indies drew the third Test at The Oval in a short three-game rubber. Captained by Wally Hammond England won the toss and elected to bat. They were finally all out for 352 with Joe Hardstaff making 94 and debutant Buddy Oldfield scoring 80. In reply West Indies hit 498 with Bam Bam Weekes scoring a cracking 137. In their second innings England made 366 for 3 declared with Len Hutton hitting an undefeated 165 and Wally Hammond 138. Unbeknown to the players and spectators it would be the last Test match for six years and two hundred and nineteen days as the Second World War began nine days later. It was also Oldfield's only Test – after the war he played only league cricket.

MONDAY 23 AUGUST 1948

James Gill completed his century on his debut in first class cricket playing for Ireland against MCC at Observatory Lane, Rathmines, Dublin. He was eventually out for 106 as Ireland made 246. When MCC batted he did not take a catch or bowl and in his second innings he was out for a duck. He never played another first class game.

THURSDAY 23 AUGUST 1984

Sri Lanka played their first Test in England at Lord's. England won the toss and decided to field. Sri Lanka made 491 for 7 before they declared with opener Sidath Wettimuny scoring 190 and captain Duleep Mendis making 111. England made 307 in return with Allan Lamb scoring 107. Sri Lanka declared their second innings on 294 for 7 with wicketkeeper-opener Amal Silva the top scorer on 102. Ian Botham took 6 for 90. England did not get an opportunity for a second innings and Wettimuny was named man of the match.

WEDNESDAY 24 AUGUST 1938

England completed the biggest ever Test victory beating the Australians by an innings and 579 runs at The Oval. England won the toss and elected to bat with Len Hutton and Bill Edrich opening for the home side. Hutton stayed at the crease for thirteen hours and seventeen minutes as he made 364 – then the highest innings in a Test match – before being out. Maurice Leyland, in his last Test, hit 187, completing a partnership of 382 with Hutton. Joe Hardstaff was 169 not out when captain Wally Hammond declared at 903 for 7. For Australia captain Don Bradman and batsman Jack Fingleton were both missing injured as the tourists tumbled to 201 all out before Hammond enforced the follow-on. They fared even less well in the second innings when they were dismissed for 123 (only one extra – a bye – added to their total).

MONDAY 24 AUGUST 1998

Sri Lankan opening batsman Russel Arnold was out for a duck twice in 75 minutes. Playing against Hampshire at Southampton who had scored 347 for 8 declared, the Sri Lankans went into bat and Arnold fell with the score on 1 before his captain declared at 39 for 4. Hampshire forfeited their second innings leaving the tourists to score 309 off 82 overs. The unfortunate Arnold completed his pair but the Sri Lankans still reached their target for the loss of only five wickets.

TUESDAY 25 AUGUST 1987

The MCC bicentenary match at Lord's – between MCC and Rest of the World XI – finished in a draw. An all-star MCC won the toss and decided to bat. When they declared with five wickets down, they had scored 455 with captain Mike Gatting scoring 179 and Graham Gooch playing in an unaccustomed number three spot hitting 117. Rest of the World XI declared their first innings at 421 for 7 with opener Sunil Gavaskar scoring a majestic 188. MCC declared at 318 for 6 in their second innings with Gordon Greenidge hitting 122 and Gooch 70. When stumps were drawn on the fourth day Rest of the World XI were on 13 for 1 which is where the match ended as there was no play on the final day.

SATURDAY 25 AUGUST 2001

Making his Test debut for England and having taken 1 for 115, James Ormond came out to bat. He was greeted by a sledging from Mark Waugh, brother of the Australian Steve, "F*** me, look who it is. Mate, what are you doing out here? There's no way you're good enough to play for England." Ormond who would be one of Shane Warne's seven victims in the match replied, "Maybe not, but at least I'm the best player in my family."

THURSDAY 26 AUGUST 1920

Percy Fender playing for Surrey against Northamptonshire at Northampton scored a century in just thirty-five minutes. It could all have been so different – Fender was dropped when he had scored just a single. It is the fastest century on record against genuine bowling.

SATURDAY 26 AUGUST 1978

On the third day of the third Test between England and New Zealand the fewest number of runs scored in a full day's first class cricket in England occurred at Lord's. Resuming at 175 for 2 with Clive Radley not out on 75 and David Gower unbeaten on 55, England made 289 all out at 4.21pm when tea was taken. Ian Botham and Bob Willis rampaged through the Kiwi batting order to leave them at 37 for 7. On day four England finished the job, bowling out New Zealand for 67 and then reaching 118 for 3 to win by 7 wickets.

TUESDAY 27 AUGUST 1889

Play was extended until 7pm on the second day of the County Championship match between Surrey and Yorkshire at The Oval. The game had been intended to last three days but a result was reached in two – thanks to the play extension Surrey won by 2 wickets. Neither captain wanted to return on the third day so they continued playing even though it was getting dark but they carried on helped by the gas lamps in nearby streets to illuminate the way.

TUESDAY 27 AUGUST 1974

Keith Fletcher completed a Test century at The Oval that he had begun on 24 August. Pakistan won the toss and decided to bat and had reached 600 for 7 when they declared with Zaheer Abbas scoring 240. England replied with 545 all out. At close of play on the third day Fletcher was 12 not out. By close of play on the fourth day he had progressed to 76 not out. By the time he reached his ton he had taken 458 minutes and 329 balls. He was finally run out for 122 and the match ended in a draw.

SATURDAY 28 AUGUST 1624

Jasper Vinall was playing cricket with friends on the green at Horsted Keynes, Sussex when he went to catch a ball hit by Edward Tye. As the ball came down Tye advanced and went to hit it again (allowed in the rules in those days) and proceeded to wallop Vinall full in the face with his bat. Jasper Vinall died on 10 September from the "mortal wound on the front of his head".

SUNDAY 28 AUGUST 2005

Big Brother contestant Vanessa Nimmo did a kiss'n'tell on Test cricketer Kevin Pietersen. They had been introduced on 4 July 2005 at the Wimbledon Gentlemen's Final. The South African-born beauty (Nimmo, not Pietersen) claimed that "sex was really dull. He is definitely just a missionary man. I think he's used to girls doing things for him." However, Pietersen had the measure of the blonde wannabe – he sent her a text message that read, "U need to realise u are a nobody trying to be a somebody".

TUESDAY 29 AUGUST 1882

The Ashes were born when English cricket "died". Australia beat England for the first time in England albeit by just seven runs. There were 39,194 spectators at the match although one died of a heart attack and another bit through his umbrella handle during the final stages. On 2 September a mock obituary appeared in *The Sporting Times* written by Reginald Brooks under the pseudonym "Bloobs" that read:

In Affectionate Remembrance
of
ENGLISH CRICKET,
which died at the Oval
on
29th AUGUST, 1882,
Deeply lamented by a large circle of sorrowing
friends and acquaintances

R.I.P.

N.B.–The body will be cremated and the
ashes taken to Australia.

The first mention of The Ashes in *Wisden Cricketers' Almanack* was in 1905, while *Wisden's* first account of the legend did not occur until the 1922 edition. There is also a dispute as to what the urn – a terracotta container six inches high that may have been a perfume jar – contains. Various theories include a stump, bail, part of a ball or even a wedding veil. However on 25 November 2006 an MCC spokesman said that it was "95 per cent" certain that the urn contains the ashes of a cricket bail.

MONDAY 29 AUGUST 2005

England (477 and 129 for 7) beat Australia (218 and 387) by three wickets in the fourth Test at Trent Bridge to take a 2-1 lead in the Ashes series.

WEDNESDAY 30 AUGUST 1899

Taking a break from writing about the world's greatest consulting detective and three years before he was knighted Arthur Conan Doyle turned out for MCC against Cambridgeshire at Lord's. He took 7 for 61 including five clean bowled. One of the Cambridgeshire team was run out while one of the other two wickets fell to Bernard Bosanquet, he creator of the googly. The match ended in a draw and 40-year-old Conan Doyle took another wicket in the second Cambridgeshire innings.

THURSDAY 31 AUGUST 1922

On the second day of the County Championship match between Nottinghamshire and Hampshire at Trent Bridge the home crowd grew restless with opposing bowler Jack Newman and began booing him. At the end of an over in which he had an appeal turned down, he threw the ball to the ground. Hampshire's captain the Honourable Lionel Tennyson ordered his man to pick up the ball but Newman refused so Tennyson sent him off. As he left Newman kicked down the stumps. In the dressing room at stumps, Tennyson said, "Jack, you have this afternoon disgraced the annals of Hampshire cricket... You must send a letter of apology. Sit down; here's pen and paper. I'll dictate the letter." Tennyson insisted that Newman write apologising to the opposing captain and the president of Nottinghamshire. Then he said, "Now, Jack, a final letter. To the Honourable L.H. Tennyson, captain, Hampshire County CC, Trent Bridge, Nottinghamshire. 'Dear Skipper, I humbly regret my behaviour, and so on', you confounded old villain; and don't let us have a repetition of your disgraceful conduct. And, good evening to you, Jack, and, damn you, take this" and gave him a five pound note.

SATURDAY 31 AUGUST 1968

At Glamorgan Gary Sobers batting for Nottingham struck bowler Malcolm Nash for six on every ball of his over. Sobers is bemused by the excitement surrounding his legendary six sixes. "Nobody talks about anything else," he said thirty years later. "At times I have to say, 'You know, it seems as though the only thing I have ever done in cricket is hit six sixes'." Sobers was captaining Nottinghamshire against Glamorgan and was about to declare, telling his batting partner John Parkin, "I think we'll have another ten minutes." Then Malcolm Nash bowled the first ball of what was to become the most famous over in cricket. Sobers walloped it out of the ground. The second ball went the way of the first, hitting the upper storey of a house in Gorse Lane, alongside the ground. When the third ball went into the members' enclosure, Glamorgan captain Tony Lewis warned Nash to play it safe. But Nash dropped the next ball short and Sobers hooked it into the crowd behind him. One of the Glamorgan slips told Sobers, "I bet you can't hit the next one for six." Sobers replied, "Ah, that's a challenge," and duly hit the ball long and high. Roger Davis caught it but fell backwards over the boundary – the previous season Sobers would have been out, but a new rule introduced earlier in 1968 meant that it was yet another six. The sixth ball landed, appropriately enough, in the garden of The Cricketers pub, where it was found the following day by a schoolboy and later presented to Sobers.

CRICKET
On This Day

SEPTEMBER

MONDAY 1 SEPTEMBER 1718

The first recorded incident of "rain stopped play" occurred at White Conduit Fields, Islington, north London in a match between London and the Rochester Punch Club Society. The match was also the first record of a cricket match involving a club side. The team from Rochester complained that "the rains, which fell so heavy, [made] it… impossible to continue the game". That was not the end of the matter and the team was taken to court at Guildhall where the Lord Chief Justice insisted that the game was completed in the following season. The winners received £60 but by the time the legal costs were taken into account the sum involved was nearly £200.

TUESDAY 1 SEPTEMBER 1891

The first inter-colonial tournament began in the West Indies in a match between Barbados and Demerara at Bay Pasture, Bridgetown, Barbados. It was a three-team tournament with Trinidad being the third. In the first match Barbados (55 and 80 for 6) beat Demerara (54 and 80) by 4 wickets. The second game was held on 4-5 September and Demerara (148 and 156 for 4 declared) beat Trinidad (92 and 61) by 151 runs. On 7-8 September Barbados (240 for 6 declared) beat Trinidad (66 and 81) by an innings and 93 runs. In the final on 9-10 September Barbados (214) beat Demerara (68 and 91) by an innings and 55 runs.

WEDNESDAY 2 SEPTEMBER 1964

The Australian tourists began a three-day match against AER Gilligan's XI at the Central Recreation Ground, Hastings. AER Gilligan's XI batted first and made 372 including 119 from Basil D'Oliveira. The Australians were all out for 281 with Jim Pressdee taking 5 for 83. AER Gilligan's XI declared their second innings on 251 for 9, Michael Norman top scoring on 81. Thanks to a century from Bill Lawry Australia made 346 for 8 to win the match by 2 wickets. It was the last first class game in which all twenty-two players took a turn at bowling.

SUNDAY 3 SEPTEMBER 1916

Kenneth Hutchings killed in action aged 33 years when he was struck by a shell at Ginchy, France. He played seven Tests for England scoring 341 runs with a top score of 126. He was serving with the King's Liverpool Regiment, attached to Welsh Regiment when he died.

SATURDAY 4 SEPTEMBER 1937

James Parks played in his last game of the 1937 season and passed 3,000 runs for the season. Playing for the Over-30s against the Under 30s Parks hit 61 to finish on 3,003 runs (average 50.89) for 1937 and he also took 101 wickets, a feat achieved by no other first class cricketer. Despite his brilliance Parks only played once for his country. In 1937 he played against New Zealand and scored just 29 runs with a high score of 22. With the ball he took 2 for 26 and 1 for 10.

SUNDAY 4 SEPTEMBER 1977

America beat West Indies at Giants' stadium in the first match played on Astroturf. Six thousand, six hundred and seventy-four people paid $50,000 to see Gary Sobers and his Caribbean All-Stars lose in an afternoon of gentle cricket. Well, perhaps not so gentle. Instead of discreet applause, tea, and the sound of leather on willow the crowd were treated to an electronic scoreboard that flashed up messages like "Give that man a hand!", "Did you see that?" and "Boing!"

TUESDAY 5 SEPTEMBER 1826

"The Little Wonder" John Wisden born in Brighton, West Sussex. He attained the height of 5ft 4in and weighed just 7 stone yet he was a demon fast bowler who took six wickets in six balls bowling underarm against 22 of United States and Canada. In 1851 he captured 455 wickets but it was for his eponymous almanack, the first edition which came out the year after he retired in 1863 that cricket lovers the world over are grateful to him.

MONDAY 6 SEPTEMBER 1880

The first Test match in England held at The Oval between England and Australia. It was the fourth Test match to be played between the two countries and England fielded eight debutants including W.G. Grace who scored the first Test century for England and his brothers Edward Mills, who faced the first ball and opened the batting with W.G. – the first instance of brothers opening a Test innings – and George Frederick. The match had originally been intended for Surrey to play Australia but club secretary Charles Alcock was instrumental in arranging the first Test match in England. W.G. Grace and Lucas shared the first century partnership (120 for the second wicket) and Australia's Billy Murdoch became the first captain to score a ton (his first in first-class cricket) as England won by 5 wickets.

SATURDAY 6 SEPTEMBER 1980

The last Gillette Cup Final held at Lord's and Middlesex beat Kent by seven wickets. Man of the match was Middlesex captain Mike Brearley who scored 96 not out. From 1981 the competition was known as the NatWest Trophy.

TUESDAY 7 SEPTEMBER 1915

Hindus beat Parsees in the Bombay Quadrangular Tournament at Deccan Gymkhana Ground, Poona. Hindus were all out for 181 with Palwankar Ganpat the top scorer on 41. With 5 for 46, M.B. Vatcha was Parsees' most successful bowler. Parsees were bowled out for 118 with S.M. Joshi taking 7 for 34. In their second innings Hindus made 178 for 7 when stumps were drawn on the second day. There was no play on the final day and the Hindus were awarded the match on first innings scores.

FRIDAY 7 SEPTEMBER 1956

The greatest all-round sportsman of all time C.B. Fry died aged 84 at the Middlesex Hospital, London, of kidney failure. At school he ran the 100 yards in less than 11 seconds and set a school long jump record of 21 feet, which was not beaten for twenty years and then only by future Olympic champion, Harold Abrahams. He played in 26 Tests but was never at his best internationally. His last first class appearances were in India in 1921-1922 and he finished with a career tally of 30,886 runs including 94 centuries at an outstanding average of 50.22. In 1920 while working for his friend Kumar Shri Ranjitsinhji at the League of Nations, Fry claimed that he was offered the kingdom of Albania. In the late 1920s and early 1930s Fry was several times struck down by mental illness. His biograher states that Fry's "stubborn conviction that he was invariably right did not always endear him to the establishment or even to his fellow journalists".

SATURDAY 7 SEPTEMBER 1963

The first Lord's cup final took place between Sussex and Worcestershire in the Gillette Cup. Sussex won the toss and decided to bat and made 168 all out in 60.2 overs (the competition was then sixty-five overs per side). Wicketkeeper Jim Parks scored 57 and debutant Norman Gifford took 4 for 33. When their turn came, Worcestershire were dismissed for 154 giving Sussex victory by 14 runs. Gifford was named the first Man of the Match in a Lord's final.

WEDNESDAY 8 SEPTEMBER 1880

The first Test match in England finished at The Oval and three Grace brothers made their Test debuts. Only W.G. really shined, scoring 152 and taking three wickets. E.M. scored 36 and 0, while George Frederick had the misfortune to become the first player in Test cricket to bag a pair – he was caught by Charles Bannerman off William Moule's bowling in the first innings when he batted at number nine and was clean bowled by Palmer when he opened England's second knock.

SATURDAY 8 SEPTEMBER 1888

At 29 Hanbury Street in London's Whitechapel district 48-year-old "Dark Annie" Chapman – so-called because she was possessed of dark wavy brown hair – became Jack the Ripper's second victim. Short (5ft) and stout, she was discovered shortly before 6am in the rear yard of 29 Hanbury Street, a three-storey house built in about 1740. Chapman's dress was pulled up over her knees and her intestines lay over her left shoulder. Her throat was cut deep to the spine and there were two cuts on the left side of the spine. Eight hours later that same day, the Blackheath Club played a cricket match against the Brothers Christopherson at Blackheath in southeast London. Playing for Blackheath that day was 31-year-old barrister and teacher Montague John Druitt who despite looking a weakling was celebrated for his great strength in his arms and wrists. He once came third in a cricket ball-throwing competition with a chuck of more than ninety-two yards. He scored 2 and took 3 wickets as the Blackheath Club won by 22 runs. Druitt was found drowned in the Thames off Thorneycroft's torpedo works, Chiswick on 31 December 1888. In 1894 Sir Melville Macnaghten, the head of CID at Scotland Yard, named Druitt as his favoured candidate for Jack the Ripper and indeed several authors have written books suggesting Druitt but substantial evidence to confirm this allegation is lacking.

SUNDAY 9 SEPTEMBER 2007

Former England captain Mike Gatting appeared as himself on an episode of radio soap *The Archers*. The episode was about a misunderstanding between Sid and Jolene Perks during the Village Cup Final at Lord's.

FRIDAY 10 SEPTEMBER 1915

Muslims scored the lowest first class innings total in India when Europeans bowled them out for 21 in the Bombay Quadrangular Tournament at Deccan Gymkhana Ground, Poona. Frank Tarrant took 5 wickets for 6 runs and Harry Simms (actually an Australian) took 4 for 2 including a hat-trick and four wickets in five balls (Feroze Khan, Yusuf Baig, Pyare Khan, Nazir Hussain). Top scorer for Muslims was Extras with 9 followed closely by Feroze Khan on eight. Europeans declared at 201 for 5 and K.A. Tamboovala took 4 for 99. Muslims fared better in the second innings making 39 but again top scorer was Extras with 15; the nearest human rival was C.M. Ali who scored an undefeated 7. Europeans won by an innings and 141 runs.

SUNDAY 10 SEPTEMBER 1989

Former West Indies captain Jeff Stollmeyer died aged 68 after being shot five times and beaten about the head by burglars at his Port-of-Spain, Trinidad home. His wife and son were also injured in the break-in. Stollmeyer was president of the West Indies Board of Control from 1974 until 1981 during which time he opposed Kerry Packer's World Series Cricket.

SATURDAY 11 SEPTEMBER 1858

Single wicket player Thomas Hunt killed after a match between 11 of England against 20 of Rochdale. Hunt decided to walk to the station to go home but foolishly walked along the tracks and was hit by a train, which cut off both his legs and the fingers of his left hand. He died from his injuries.

TUESDAY 11 SEPTEMBER 2001

Guyanese batsman Nezam Ahmed Hafiz murdered aged 32 in the terrorist attack on New York's World Trade Center. He played half a dozen matches for Guyana before migrating to America where he became captain of the American Cricket Society and the Commonwealth League and represented his adopted state New York in local tournaments. He toured England with the USA national side in 2000. He worked on the 94th floor of Tower One for insurance company Marsh and McLennan.

THURSDAY 12 SEPTEMBER 1901

C.B. Fry hit 105 for Rest of England against Yorkshire at Lord's to become the first batsman to score six consecutive centuries in first class cricket. The Rest of England won by an innings and 115 runs.

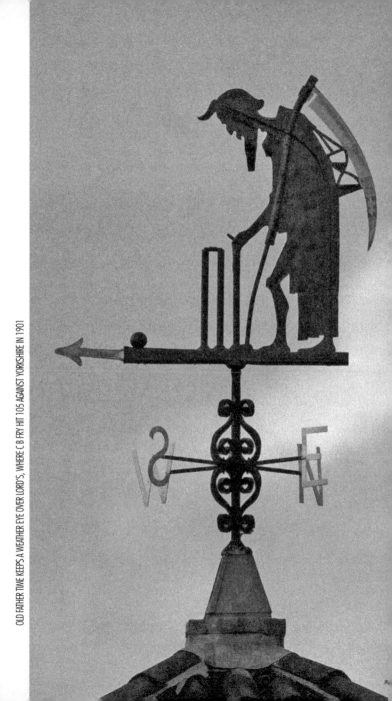

MONDAY 12 SEPTEMBER 2005

South African-born Englishman Kevin Pietersen scored an Ashes-winning 158 for England against Australia at The Oval and included seven sixes in his knock, one more than Ian Botham hit during his Ashes-winning performance in 1981. Although the match ended in a draw, England regained the Ashes by already being 2-1 up in the series.

MONDAY 13 SEPTEMBER 1915

Europeans met Hindus in the final of the Bombay Quadrangular Tournament at Deccan Gymkhana Ground, Poona. Hindus won the toss, decided to bat and scored 201 all out. In reply Europeans made 269 all out with Frank Tarrant the top scorer on 52. Hindus were dismissed for 138 in their second innings with Tarrant taking 5 wickets for 41. Tarrant and Kenneth Goldie scored 71 to win the match and the tournament for Europeans by 10 wickets.

TUESDAY 13 SEPTEMBER 2005

After several unsuccessful applications and a five-year wait Rhodesia-born England coach Duncan Fletcher was granted a passport – no doubt on the back of England's success at regaining the Ashes. The same day the victorious team toured the streets of London and Freddie Flintoff told commentator David Gower that he had not yet been to bed.

MONDAY 14 SEPTEMBER 1903

The first match between the winners of the County Championship and a team made up of The Rest played at The Oval. Champions Middlesex drew.

SUNDAY 14 SEPTEMBER 1997

During a Sahara Cup game between India and Pakistan at Toronto, Inzamam-ul-Haq, the Pakistani batsman, interrupted play for 35 minutes when he became angry with spectator Shiv Kumar Thind, 29, calling him a potato through a megaphone. Inzaman strode off the pitch pausing only to collect a bat from Pakistan's 12th man, Mushtaq Ahmed, and threatened the hapless Thind. An eyewitness said, "If not for the spectators and security staff curbing him, he would have broken the head of that guy. The guy with the megaphone was no match for Inzamam and got mauled. Even when Canadian police took Inzamam back on to the field, he was trying to get back to the stands." The

Canadian police watched the incident on video and arrested Inzamam and charged him with two charges of assault and one of assault with a deadly weapon. Eventually Thind dropped the charges but match referee Jackie Hendriks suspended Inzamam for two One Day Internationals.

MONDAY 15 SEPTEMBER 1975

Chris Balderstone became the only man to play first class cricket and first class football on the same day. He played for Leicestershire against Derbyshire at Queen's Park, Chesterfield and was on 51 when bad light stopped play. That evening he turned out in midfield for Doncaster Rovers in a 1-1 draw against Brentford in the Fourth Division. When that match had finished, he played darts for Doncaster Rovers players' team against a supporters' team in the Rovers supporters' club. The following day he resumed his innings and was finally run out for 116.

THURSDAY 15 SEPTEMBER 2005

Nottinghamshire opener Jason Gallian became the only batsman to be run out for 199, not only twice in a career but also in the same season. The first instance was against Sussex in April at Nottingham and the second occurrence was today against Kent at Canterbury.

FRIDAY 16 SEPTEMBER 1910

Former Essex slow bowler and *Wisden* Cricketer of the Year in 1898 Fred Bull tied a seven-pound stone around his neck, sat down in the water, and drowned himself at St Anne's-on-Sea, Lancashire. He was 35. When he was awarded the *Wisden* accolade, the almanack editor wrote, "Presuming he does not get over-worked there seems to be a very brilliant career before him."

THURSDAY 16 SEPTEMBER 2004

A boozy punch-up followed Australia's seven-wicket victory over New Zealand at The Oval in the ICC Champions Trophy. Australia won the toss and decided to field. The Kiwis made 198 for 9 in their fifty overs but Australia easily overhauled the total for the loss of just three wickets. As the winning run was struck a dozen drunks invaded the pitch followed by a similar number of stewards. It took twenty minutes for order to be restored – Aussie captain Ricky Ponting blamed it on "too many beers in the sun".

SATURDAY 17 SEPTEMBER 1988

Yorkshire beat Nottinghamshire by 127 runs at Trent Bridge in the County Championship. At the start of the match – the last of the season – Franklyn Stephenson of Nottinghamshire needed 210 to complete the double of 1,000 runs and 100 wickets in the season. Up to then Stephenson had never scored a century for his county so it looked unlikely that he would reach his target. He needed no further encouragement to enter the record books. He hit 111 in the first innings in 157 minutes and 117 in the second innings. He also took 4 for 105 and 7 for 117 to become only the third player in first class cricket to score two centuries and take ten wickets in the same match.

SATURDAY 17 SEPTEMBER 2005

Nottinghamshire won the County Championship for the fifth time in their history, having won the Division 2 title the previous year.

THURSDAY 18 SEPTEMBER 1997

Zimbabwe met New Zealand at Harare Sports Club in the first Test to feature three pairs of brothers in one team: Andy and Grant Flower, Bryan and Paul Strang, and Gavin and John Rennie for Zimbabwe. Guy Whittall was also in the team; his cousin Andy was 12th man. The match was drawn.

TUESDAY 18 SEPTEMBER 2001

Australian left-hander Barry Shepherd died aged 64. He played in nine Tests in the 1960s but never managed to score a ton – his best was 96 against South Africa on 3 January 1964. He was captain of Western Australia but retired aged 28 to work in finance and later in cricket administration. He was awarded the Order of Australia Medal in 1999.

SATURDAY 19 SEPTEMBER 1998

South Africa won the only gold medal for cricket in the Commonwealth Games when they beat Australia by four wickets in Kuala Lumpur. Four years earlier, the Ministry of Education in Malaysia had introduced cricket to the school curriculum in the hope of a good showing. However, the semi finals were contested by four giants South Africa v Sri Lanka and Australia v New Zealand. The Springboks won the toss and elected to field. With three balls of their allotted fifty overs to go, Australia were bowled out for 183 thanks in no small part to captain Steve Waugh who scored an unbeaten 90. Springbok captain Shaun Pollock (following in the Test footsteps of his father Peter and Uncle Graeme) took 4 for 19. South Africa needed 184 from fifty overs and managed to reach that total with four overs to spare. Mike Rindel was the top scorer with 67.

SATURDAY 20 SEPTEMBER 1902

A culinary cricket contest at Lord's had the City Cooks playing the West End Waiters. The waiters wore evening dress while the cooks wore chef's whites. One newspaper reported, "The game was in no sense intended to be comic, for the teams played with a keenness which is seldom, if ever, seen on a cricket field. To the spectators, however, the proceedings were a huge joke, so much so that he the players became irritated at the universal hilarity."

SUNDAY 20 SEPTEMBER 1931

The first black Test cricketer Sam Morris died aged 76 at Albert Park, Melbourne, Victoria. He was likely the son of West Indians who had gone to Tasmania for the gold rush in the 1850s. He made his Test debut (his only game) in the second game of the 1884-1885 rubber after the Australian team had refused to play in an argument over gate money. He opened the batting in Australia's first innings and scored 4; he was 10 not out in the second innings although he batted at number ten. He took 2 for 73 (the wickets of Arthur Shrewsbury and Billy Barnes) and was excellent in the field. However, England won by 10 wickets and he was not selected again. He was a regular for Victoria until 1892-1893. He retired in 1898 as his eyesight was failing and he became a groundsman. He had to stop that too in 1910 when he went completely blind.

SATURDAY 21 SEPTEMBER 1901

Cricket's first peer Learie Constantine born at Petit Valley, Diego Martin, near Maraval, Trinidad. His father toured England twice with West Indies (1900, 1906) and the two men played together only once in 1922. The following year, Constantine was picked to tour England but he was chosen for his fielding rather than any ability with bat or ball. In eighteen Test matches he averaged 19.24 with the bat and 30.10 with the ball. He became Trinidad's first high commissioner in London (1961) and a knighthood followed in the 1962 New Year's Honours List. Constantine served on two newly created bodies, the Sports Council (1965) and the Race Relations Board (1966), and was elected rector of St Andrews University in 1967. A life peerage came in 1969, two years before his death at the age of 69.

SUNDAY 21 SEPTEMBER 1997

Pakistan beat India in the fifth one day international in the Sahara "Friendship" Cup at Toronto Cricket, Skating and Curling Club but still lost the series 4-1. India made 250 for 5 from their fifty overs and Sourav Ganguly top scored with 96. Owing to a slow over rate, Pakistan were fined two overs and their target had to be reached in 48 overs. They made it for the loss of five wickets and with 37 balls to spare.

WEDNESDAY 22 SEPTEMBER 1880

Fred Grace, the youngest of the international playing Grace brothers, died of pneumonia aged 29 a fortnight after he had made his Test debut against Australia at The Oval – albeit an inauspicious one when he bagged a pair.

MONDAY 22 SEPTEMBER 1986

A Test was tied for only the second time in 1,052 matches. India played Australia at M.A. Chidambaram Stadium, Chepauk, Madras and Australia won the toss and decided to bat. Australia made 574 for 7 when captain Allan Border declared. Dean Jones had scored 210, David Boon 122 and Border himself 106. India were bowled out for 397 with captain Kapil Dev scoring 119. Greg Matthews took 5 for 103. Border surprised many by declaring the second Australian knock on 170 for 5 leaving India 348 to win in 87 overs. The Indians set about their task with skill and pace – but at 5.18pm with one run needed for victory in the fifth ball of Greg Matthews's 40th over he trapped the Indian number eleven Maninder Singh lbw leaving the scores tied, both teams having scored 744 runs.

SATURDAY 23 SEPTEMBER 1876

The first England touring team – James Lillywhite's XI – sailed from Southampton aboard the SS Poonah bound for New Zealand and Australia. The squad of twelve faced a six-month tour for which they were offered £200 each. It wasn't enough to persuade some leading figures such as W.G. Grace so they stayed at home.

SUNDAY 23 SEPTEMBER 1979

Pressure got to Australian fast bowler Rodney Hogg on the second day of the second Test between India and Australia at Karnataka State Cricket

Association Stadium, Bangalore. Apparently unable to dislodge Dilip Vengsarkar and Gundappa Viswanath and having been no-balled 11 times in six overs Hogg bowled a beamer, kicked over the stumps and left the pitch. Hogg was saved from disciplinary action by his captain Kim Hughes who immediately apologised and persuaded Hogg to do likewise.

TUESDAY 24 SEPTEMBER 1844

The first international outside Britain – United States of America v Canada – began at St George's Club Ground, New York, United States of America. The United States of America won the toss and decided to field. Canada made 82 with Sheffield-born Sam Wright taking five wickets. Henry Groom took three wickets and he bowled the first ball to D. Winckworth. The USA scored 64, one more than Canada's second innings total. Groom took seven wickets. When bad weather prevented play on the second day, it was agreed to extend the match into a third day. The USA were dismissed for 58 in their second innings resulting in a Canadian win by 23 runs and they collected a $1,000 prize. Four years earlier, Toronto and St George's of New York played in the first match between teams from different countries. St George's won the match in New York by ten wickets. Players from both teams represented their respective countries in 1844.

SATURDAY 24 SEPTEMBER 1859

The first match on the first cricket tour began – 22 of Lower Canada faced 11 of England at Montreal. One of the 11 of England was John Wisden and the tourists – all twelve of them – left Liverpool on 7 September. Battling rough seas, mal de mer, icebergs, fog and storms, they docked at Quebec on 22 September. They won their first game by eight wickets and went on to win their four remaining fixtures. They travelled more than 7,500 miles in two months and left for England on 11 November. The organiser of the tour, Fred Lillywhite, later published the first book account of an overseas tour, *The English Cricketers' Trip To Canada And The United States In 1859*.

WEDNESDAY 25 SEPTEMBER 1771

The Hambledon Club announced that the bat must be no wider than four and a quarter inches. The pronouncement came after Thomas White batted with a blade as wide as the wicket.

SATURDAY 25 SEPTEMBER 1915

Britain's best schoolboy cricketer John Howell killed at Flanders, aged 20. In consecutive innings in 1913 he hit 108, 114 and 144. The following year, 1914, he scored two innings of 202 each against Old Reptonians and Uppingham. At the outbreak of war he joined the King's Royal Corps and was a 2nd Lieutenant at the time of his death.

MONDAY 26 SEPTEMBER 1977

The High Court hearing began between Tony Greig, Mike Proctor and John Snow and the TCCB with the cricketers claiming that their ban on playing because they had signed for Kerry Packer's World Series Cricket (WSC) was an unfair restraint of trade. The hearing lasted 31 days, the judgment, occupying 221 foolscap pages, took Mr. Justice Slade five and a half hours to deliver. He ruled in favour of Greig, the other players and WSC and the defendants were ordered to pay the costs.

SUNDAY 26 SEPTEMBER 1999

Indian slow left-armer Sunil Joshi took five South African wickets at Gymkhana Club Ground, Nairobi in the LG Cup to return figures of 10-6-6-5, the fourth most economical in one day international history. His victims were Boeta Dippenaar, Herschelle Gibbs, Hansie Cronje, Jonty Rhodes and Shaun Pollock. India won by eight wickets with over 27 overs to spare.

TUESDAY 27 SEPTEMBER 1927

Charles Newhall, the fastest bowler of his time in the USA, died aged 80. With his brothers he had been instrumental in establishing cricket in Philadelphia after the Civil War. He habitually went into bat carrying a lemon, which he would suck between strokes. It had another use – if a wicketkeeper appealing too loudly annoyed him he would spit the citric acid into the unfortunate glovesman's eyes.

TUESDAY 27 SEPTEMBER 1983

Eddie Hemmings became the only bowler to take all ten wickets in a first-class match in the West Indies; he took 10 for 175 while playing for an International XI against West Indies XI at Sabina Park, Kingston in the Shell/Air Florida Cricket Festival. The West Indies XI made 419 and Hemmings's was the most expensive ten-wicket bowling analysis in first class cricket.

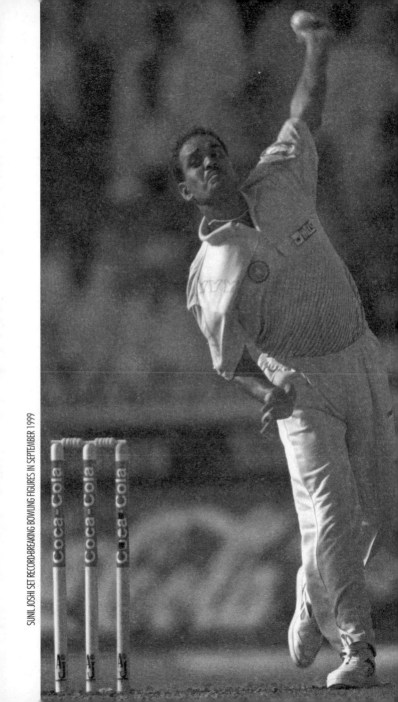

SUNIL JOSHI SET RECORD-BREAKING BOWLING FIGURES IN SEPTEMBER 1999

SUNDAY 28 SEPTEMBER 1884

England's fastest bowler of his time Fred Morley died of congestion and dropsy aged 33. He made his Test debut in 1880 and played in three matches in England's tour of 1882-1883 but on the outward journey he cracked a rib when the ship was involved in a collision in Colombo harbour. He never fully recovered.

FRIDAY 28 SEPTEMBER 1984

The first floodlit one-day international outside Australia took place at Jawaharlal Nehru Stadium, New Delhi between India and Australia. The tourists made 220 for 9 with opener Kepler Wessels scoring 107. India were all out for 172 and Australia won by 48 runs.

MONDAY 29 SEPTEMBER 1941

Unlikely Test hero David Steele born at Bradeley, Staffordshire. His first class career was nearing its end when Tony Greig picked him for England in 1975 and in eight matches Steele scored 673 runs with a top score of 106. He was not known for being a spendthrift especially in the bar after a match and his teammates nicknamed him "Crime" because crime never pays.

THURSDAY 29 SEPTEMBER 1983

India's opener Aunshuman Gaekwad completed the slowest double century in Tests, against Pakistan at Burlton Park, Jullundur. He took 652 minutes and 426 balls to reach his milestone as the second Test fizzled out into a draw. In his final tally of 201 he hit 17 fours and no sixes.

TUESDAY 30 SEPTEMBER 1969

After rioting in Ahmedabad forced the location of the first Test between India and New Zealand to be changed to Brabourne Stadium, Bombay, spinners Bishan Bedi and Erapalli Prasanna's bowling skill dismissed the Kiwis for 127 short of their victory target of 188.

FRIDAY 30 SEPTEMBER 1994

Australia's opening batsman Mark Taylor became the first player to bag a pair in his first Test as captain when he played against Pakistan at National Stadium, Karachi. To add to his woes, Pakistan won by one wicket.

CRICKET
On This Day

OCTOBER

WEDNESDAY 1 OCTOBER 1997

The first one day international, Zimbabwe v New Zealand ended in a tie – the thirteenth since ODIs began – at Queens Sports Club, Bulawayo. Kiwi Chris Harris needed two runs from the last ball to win the match, but as he drove it past the bowler John Rennie the crowd rushed onto the pitch. Craig Evans beat the throng to the ball – had it reached them the Kiwis would have won – and ran out Gavin Larsen as he attempted a second run.

SUNDAY 1 OCTOBER 2000

Zimbabwe beat New Zealand at Queens Sports Club, Bulawayo by six wickets to win the three-match series 2-1. The Kiwis made 264 for 8 from their fifty overs. In reply Alistair Campbell hit an unbeaten 99 as Zimbabwe made 268 for 4 with 13 balls to spare. The total was Zimbabwe's highest when batting second at home to win an ODI.

FRIDAY 2 OCTOBER 1964

South Africa scored the most runs in a single day in first class cricket in South Africa when they hit 618 for 4 against The Rest of South Africa at New Wanderers Stadium, Johannesburg. Four Springboks – Colin Bland, Graeme Pollock, Tony Pithey and Denis Lindsay – scored centuries as South Africa won by an innings and 135 runs.

THURSDAY 2 OCTOBER 1997

Set 217 to win in 49 overs in Lahore, Pakistan easily beat India reaching 219 for 1 in 26.2 overs to win by nine wickets with 136 balls remaining. Ijaz Ahmed hit 139 not out off 84 balls, with 10 fours and nine sixes.

TUESDAY 3 OCTOBER 1905

The man with two Test careers Errol Ashton Clairmonte Hunte was born at Port-of-Spain, Trinidad. An opening batsman and wicketkeeper, on 11 January 1930 he played for West Indies against an England team captained by the Honourable F. S. G. Calthorpe but oddly Hunte went into bat at number eleven. When he was selected for the second Test he resumed his usual position and opened the batting but was listed for many years as R.L. Hunte because a copy typist misheard Errol as R.L. To add to the confusion, in MCC's next game against British Guiana at Georgetown, the bowling was opened by none other than 46-year-old R.L. (Ronald Lionel) Hunte. The records were not amended until 1967, the year that he died.

SATURDAY 3 OCTOBER 1998

Rugby-playing cricketer Arthur Clues died aged 74. He played rugby league for Leeds and Australia and turned out for Leeds Cricket Club. He is believed to be the only man to score a try and a century at Headingley.

SATURDAY 4 OCTOBER 1975

East African cricketer Don Pringle killed aged 43 in a car crash four months after representing his adopted country in the first World Cup. A landscape consultant he moved to Kenya in the 1950s and his son the future Essex and England player Derek was born there in 1958. Don Pringle played in two of East Africa's three World Cup matches. He died on the way home from a cricket match in Nairobi in which he'd taken 6 for 16.

SUNDAY 4 OCTOBER 1992

Pakistan beat India in the first Hong Kong Sixes Final, held at Kowloon Cricket Club. Wasim Akram was named as Player of the Tournament. Pakistan also won the title in 1997, 2001 and 2002.

SATURDAY 5 OCTOBER 1811

Sydney Cricket Ground mentioned in print for the first time by the local paper *Sydney Gazette*.

WEDNESDAY 5 OCTOBER 2005

The so-called Super Series Internationals began in Melbourne. The ICC idea was to pit the best in the world, then Australia, against the rest of the world, ICC World XI. The ICC arranged three one day internationals and one Test match. However, the series was so one-sided with Australia easily winning that the idea to hold the series every four years was quickly abandoned.

MONDAY 6 OCTOBER 1930

Australian all-rounder turned television commentator Richie Benaud born at Perth, New South Wales. *Wisden* Cricketer of the Year in 1962, he made his Test debut ten years earlier on 25 January 1952 against West Indies and appeared in 63 Tests scoring 2,201 runs with a top score of 122. He took 248 wickets with his best figures being 7 for 72. His last broadcast in England was near the end of the final day of the fifth Test at The Oval in 2005. His last words were "[Glenn] McGrath got his man [Kevin Pietersen], and up in the commentary box now, Mark Nicholas and Tony Greig."

SUNDAY 6 OCTOBER 1946

The 6ft 6in England captain who turned his back on his adoptive country Tony Greig born at Queenstown, Cape Province, South Africa. He was instrumental in the setting up of Kerry Packer's WSC circus. Greig played 58 Tests for England between June 1972 and August 1977. He was *Wisden* Cricketer of the Year in 1975.

FRIDAY 7 OCTOBER 1988

England cancelled the proposed winter tour of India after the Indian government refused to grant visas to eight of the touring party whose names appeared on a list of sportsmen with links to South Africa. The proscribed eight included captain Graham Gooch and vice-captain John Emburey.

TUESDAY 7 OCTOBER 2008

Former Test captian Sourav Ganguly said the forthcoming rubber against Australia would be his last. He added, "To be honest, I don't expect to be picked for this series." As it turned out he played in all four Tests but ended his international career with a golden duck.

TUESDAY 8 OCTOBER 1872

God-fearing Leicestershire and England batsman Albert Knight was born at Leicester. *Wisden* Cricketer of the Year in 1904, he made almost four hundred first class appearances but only appeared in three Tests. He had a habit of going down on his knees at the crease before each innings to ask for almighty assistance. In one match the appeal irritated Lancashire fast bowler Walter Brearley who complained to the umpire that Knight was receiving unfair help.

WEDNESDAY 8 OCTOBER 1969

New Zealand (319 and 214) beat India (257 and 109) by 167 runs at Vidarbha Cricket Association Ground, Nagpur to attain their first Test win on the subcontinent. Hedley Howarth took 5 for 34 from 23 overs in India's second knock.

FRIDAY 9 OCTOBER 1789

The Honourable Colonel Charles Lennox scored the first known century in Scotland when he hit 136 not out at Aberdeen playing for Gordon Castle against 55th Regiment.

MONDAY 9 OCTOBER 1995

The only British prime minister who played first class cricket Lord Home of the Hirsel died aged 92. As Lord Dunglass, he played for Eton and scored 66 in the annual match against Harrow. He played ten first-class matches for six different teams including Oxford University, Middlesex and MCC. Gradually, politics became more important to him and he became an MP in 1931, becoming foreign secretary and prime minister in 1963 on the resignation of Harold Macmillan.

FRIDAY 10 OCTOBER 2003

Having ignored W.G. Grace's maxim Zimbabwe watched as Australia declared their innings on 735 for 6 at Western Australia Cricket Association Ground, Perth with Matthew Hayden scoring 380 to break Brian Lara's record of the highest individual Test total. Hayden faced 437 balls in 622 minutes and hit 38 fours and 11 sixes. Wicketkeeper Adam Gilchrist scored 113. Zimbabwe were all out for 239 and invited to follow on and made 321 but still lost by an innings and 175 runs. And Grace's maxim? "When you win the toss, bat. If you are in doubt, think about it, then bat. If you have very big doubts, consult a colleague – then bat."

SATURDAY 11 OCTOBER 1902

The first Test between South Africa and Australia began at Old Wanderers, Johannesburg. The Aussies had not long finished a tour of England and were mentally unprepared for the match. The Springboks with six debutants made 454; then bowled out Australia for 296, forcing the follow on. A magnificent 142 from Clem Hill saved the tourists and the match was drawn.

THURSDAY 11 OCTOBER 1956

A slow day in Test cricket as Pakistan played Australia for the first time and bowled out the Aussies for just 80 and then made 15 for 2 by the time stumps were drawn to make the slowest day of Test cricket. The match was played on matting at the National Stadium in Karachi and Fazal Mahmood (6 for 34) and Khan Mohammad (4 for 43) destroyed the Australian line-up captained by Ian Johnson and including Colin McDonald, Neil Harvey, Keith Miller, Richie Benaud, Alan Davidson and Ray Lindwall. On the second day Pakistan were bowled out for 199 with Johnson taking 4 for 50. In their second innings Australia made 187 with Benaud top scoring with 56. It wasn't enough and Pakistan scored 69 for 1 to win by nine wickets.

MONDAY 12 OCTOBER 1936

Bowler Bernard Bosanquet died at his home in Wykehurst, Ewhurst, Surrey, the day before his 59th birthday. To cricket fans he is remembered for inventing the googly about which he wrote, "Poor old googly! It has been subjected to ridicule, abuse, contempt, incredulity, and survived them all. Deficiencies existing at the present day are attributed to the influence of the googly. If the standard of bowling falls off it is because too many cricketers devote their time to trying to master it." An off-break bowled with a leg-break action, it is known as a Bosie in Australia. Non-cricket fans know him, if at all, as the father of bibulous newsreader Reginald Bosanquet (1932-1984).

SATURDAY 12 OCTOBER 2002

New Zealand cricketer Mark Parker died at Bali of wounds received in the 2002 bombings, carried out by Muslim terrorists Jemaah Islamiyah. The son and nephew of cricketers, Parker captained New Zealand at Under-20 level and was celebrating his 27th birthday when he was caught in the carnage.

THURSDAY 13 OCTOBER 2005

Left-handed batsman Sourav Ganguly sacked as captain of the Indian one day team and replaced by Rahul Dravid. He had played 311 One Day Internationals for his country.

FRIDAY 13 OCTOBER 2006

Exiled Zimbabwe cricketer Henry Olonga won the final of Five's *The All Star Talent Show* with 50 per cent of the overall votes for his operatic singing. In his heat he had seen off the challenges of lesbian activist Rhona Cameron (jazz singing), former soap star Kevin Kennedy (singing), singers The Cheeky Girls (ballet dancing), socialite Princess Tamara Czartoryska (flamenco dancing) and TV presenter Jeremy Beadle (performing magic tricks). In the final Olonga beat TV presenter Roy Walker (also singing opera), TV presenter Toby Anstis (jazz dancing), model Jodie Marsh (Latin dancing), journalists Carol Thatcher (tap dancing) and Juliette Foster (singing).

SATURDAY 14 OCTOBER 1989

Pakistani Wasim Akram captured the wickets of Jeff Dujon, Malcolm Marshall and Curtly Ambrose at Sharjah Cricket Association Stadium to take the fourth hat-trick in One Day Internationals. Pakistan won the match by eleven runs.

THURSDAY 14 OCTOBER 1999

India and New Zealand drew the first Test at Punjab Cricket Association Stadium, Mohali, Chandigarh. On day one New Zealand bowled India out for 83 with Dion Nash taking 6 for 27. The Kiwis replied with 215 as Javagal Srinath took 6 for 45. In their second knock India made 505 for 3 declared leaving the Kiwis needing 374 for a win. They were 251 for 7 at stumps and pleased to have avoided the defeat.

TUESDAY 15 OCTOBER 1857

John Grange of Dacre Banks met James Sadler of Leeds in a single wicket competition at Victoria Ground, Woodhouse Moor, Leeds, beginning at 11.45am with £50 at stake. Both men were allowed a fielder. Grange batted first and scored 17 plus 10 wides from 159 balls in two and a half hours. Unlike the usual 22 yards, to get a run the batsman had to cover a distance of 40 yards. Sadler scored 24 off 93 balls when the first day ended. Grange made 21 on the second day before rain stopped play. He reached 24 before he was out caught and bowled. In his second innings Sadler made just three before Grange's fielder caught him.

THURSDAY 15 OCTOBER 1964

Sussex and former England captain Ted Dexter contested the Cardiff South East seat for the Conservatives in the General Election. Dexter was standing against Jim Callaghan, the sitting member, in a two-horse race and managed to win 22,288 votes – 42.52 per cent of the votes cast – but it was not enough as "Sunny Jim" retained his seat with 30,129 or 57.48 per cent of the votes. Callaghan had a majority of 7,841. The result saw the end of thirteen years of Tory rule and the new Prime Minister Harold Wilson appointed Callaghan as Chancellor of the Exchequer.

THURSDAY 16 OCTOBER 1952

Hanif Mohammad made his debut in Test Matches and also became the youngest wicketkeeper when he appeared in Pakistan's first official Test, against India at Feroz Shah Kotla, Delhi. India won the toss, decided to bat and made 372. Pakistan were all out for 150 with Mohammad scoring 51. Following on, they were dismissed for 152, which meant India won by an innings and 70 runs. Mohammad let 28 byes go past him and in a Test career that would last for 55 matches only kept wicket in the first three.

SATURDAY 16 OCTOBER 1976

New Zealand beat Pakistan by just one run in the only one day international of the tour at Jinnah Stadium, Sialkot. New Zealand won the toss and decided to bat. They made 198 for 8 from their 35 overs with captain and man of the match Glenn Turner hitting 67. Pakistan replied with 197 for 9 against the Kiwis who had four debutants in their side.

MONDAY 17 OCTOBER 2005

Australia beat ICC World XI in the first and only Test, held at Sydney Cricket Ground. Australia had already easily won three limited overs internationals and having won the toss, decided to bat. Australia made 345 with 111 from Matthew Hayden and 94 from Adam Gilchrist. Freddie Flintoff took 4 for 59. In their first innings ICC World XI were all out for 190, only Virender Sehwag with 76 put up any real resistance to the Aussies. Stuart MacGill took 4 for 39. Australia made 199 in their second innings. ICC World XI were all out for 144 and MacGill was again top bowler with 5 for 43. Much to the embarrassment of the ICC the match was scheduled for six days but finished in four and had it not been for the rain and bad light, it could have been over in three.

FRIDAY 17 OCTOBER 2008

At 2.31pm at the Punjab Cricket Association Stadium, Mohali, Chandigarh, Sachin Tendulkar scored three runs off Australia's Peter Siddle to become the highest run scorer in Test cricket, breaking Brian Lara's record, which had stood for nearly two years. Later in the game Tendulkar hit a half-century to become the first player to score 12,000 runs in the Test arena. Coincidentally, Lara, too, achieved the world record against Australia.

SUNDAY 18 OCTOBER 1992

Zimbabwe played its first Test match thus becoming the ninth Test-playing nation, meeting India at Harare. The game ended in a draw. Zimbabwe has not played Test cricket since 18 January 2006 because of the political situation under the tyrannical Robert Mugabe.

SATURDAY 18 OCTOBER 1969

New Zealand had a successful day at Lal Bahadur Shastri Stadium, Hyderabad, Deccan bowling out India for 89. The pitch, which the groundsman forgot to mow and Kiwi captain Graham Dowling refused to allow him to rectify, helped them. At one stage India were 49 for 9 before Srinivasaraghavan Venkataraghavan (25 not out) and Bishan Bedi (20) put on 40 for the last wicket. As Bedi was out caught Dowling off Bev Congdon's bowling the crowd went wild and began to lob stones at the police, light bonfires in the stand and set fire to the roof. Play was abandoned twenty minutes early.

WEDNESDAY 19 OCTOBER 1859

Sir Francis Lacey, the first man to be knighted for services to cricket, born at Wareham, Dorset. He played football and cricket for Cambridge, obtaining a Blue for football in 1881 and one for cricket in 1882. A barrister by profession, he played for Hampshire and from 1898 to 1926 he was secretary of MCC. On his retirement, he became the first man to be knighted for services to any sport.

THURSDAY 19 OCTOBER 1989

England beat Australia by 7 wickets with 15 balls remaining at Lal Bahadur Shastri Stadium, Hyderabad, Deccan in the second match of the MRF World Series (Nehru Cup). The Aussies fresh from a 4-0 Ashes victory the previous summer won the toss and made 242 for 3 with Allan Border hitting 84 off 44 balls, including three successive sixes off Gladstone Small. England got off to a great start with an opening stand of 185 between captain Graham Gooch and Wayne Larkins before Gooch was out lbw to that man Border. He also caught Larkins for 124 before Robin Smith and Alec Stewart saw England through to victory.

FRIDAY 20 OCTOBER 1995

Sri Lanka beat West Indies in the Sharjah final to win the Singer Champions Trophy – their first one-day series involving more than two teams. Sri Lanka made 273 all out with opener Roshan Mahanama hitting 66 from 103 balls. The first three batsmen all hit 50 or more. West Indies never really seemed in the running and were dismissed for 223.

SUNDAY 20 OCTOBER 1996

In the first Test against Zimbabwe at Sheikhupura Stadium Wasim Akram hit 257 not out, the highest score by a number eight in Tests. His mammoth innings included a record dozen sixes and 22 fours. The match ended in a draw.

MONDAY 21 OCTOBER 1940

Cantankerous opening batsman Geoff Boycott born at Fitzwilliam, near Wakefield, Yorkshire. In his first full season (1963) playing for Yorkshire Boycs scored 1,628 runs averaging more than 45. A year later, he was opening for England against Australia at Trent Bridge and scored his first Test century in the fifth Test of the rubber. He was *Wisden* Cricketer of the Year in 1965. In 1971 he became captain of Yorkshire but he was not universally popular and in September 1978 the committee sacked him. He chose not to play for England for thirty Tests because, some believed, he thought that he should have been appointed captain instead of Mike Denness in succession to Ray Illingworth. Michael Atherton described Boycott's politics was being "to the right of Genghis Khan". His critics picked up on the fact that his self-imposed exile coincided with the time that Lillee and Thomson were at their fastest. Lillee said of him, "Geoffrey is the only fellow I've ever met who fell in love with himself at a young age and has remained faithful ever since."

MONDAY 21 OCTOBER 1991

Pakistan (236 for 7: Rameez Raja 90, Imran Khan 77; Curtly Ambrose 5 for 53) beat West Indies (235: Richie Richardson 122, Jeff Dujon 53; Waqar Younis 4 for 39) by one run in the Wills Sharjah Trophy one day international at Sharjah Cricket Association Stadium.

SUNDAY 22 OCTOBER 1989

Having been the first batsman to be dismissed for handling the ball in One Day Internationals Mohinder Amarnath of India became the second player in ODIs to be out for obstructing the field. He was playing at Gujarat Stadium, Motera, Ahmedabad against Sri Lanka and was on 28 when he kicked a ball away from the bowler to prevent being run out. Still, India won by 6 runs (see 9 February 1986).

SUNDAY 22 OCTOBER 1989

England opener Graham Gooch turned bowling sensation to take 3 for 19 (including Wasim Akram first ball) at Barabati Stadium, Cuttack in the Nehru Cup match against Pakistan. England won by four wickets.

SATURDAY 23 OCTOBER 1915

The Grand Old Man of cricket W.G. Grace died at Fairmount, his home in Mottingham, Kent. Cause of death is variously ascribed to a heart attack, a stroke or a brain haemorrhage. He was buried three days later at Elmers End cemetery in London. He left £7,278 10/1d.

THURSDAY 23 OCTOBER 2008

The life ban imposed on Saleem Malik by the Pakistan Cricket Board lifted. A former Pakistan captain, he had been banned for alleged match fixing in May 2000, a year and four months after he played his last Test match. Australian bowler Shane Warne had sworn an affidavit that during the Karachi Test in 1994 Malik had offered him A$200,000 to bowl badly on the final day of the match.

FRIDAY 24 OCTOBER 1969

Hanif Mohammad and his brother Sadiq opened the innings for Pakistan against New Zealand at National Stadium, Karachi – it would be Hanif's last Test and Sadiq's first. They were the first set of brothers to open a Test innings since E.M. and W.G. Grace at The Oval for England against Australia in 1880 and like England in 1880 there was a third brother playing that match – Mushtaq Mohammad batted at number four.

SUNDAY 24 OCTOBER 1976

Sadiq and Mushtaq Mohammad (the captain) became the second set of brothers – after Ian and Greg Chappell – to score a century in the same Test match when they made tons in the second Test against New Zealand at Niaz Stadium, Hyderabad.

MONDAY 25 OCTOBER 1982

On the fourth and final day of the Sheffield Shield match between South Australia and Victoria at the Adelaide Oval South Australia captain David Hookes scored a century off just 34 deliveries. South Australia won the toss and Hookes decided to field. Victoria were dismissed for 260 with West Indian pace man Joel Garner taking four wickets. In their first innings South Australia made 409, which included centuries from Hookes (137) and former Test batsman John Inverarity (126). Victoria's Peter King took 5 for 88. In reply, Victoria made 420 for 9 declared with 151 coming from captain Graham Yallop. Hookes opened the second innings and scored a 50 in just 17 balls faced in 17 minutes. His ton came after 34 balls and 43 minutes and included 17 fours and three sixes. Despite the brilliant stroke play from the South Australia captain the match ended in a draw.

MONDAY 25 OCTOBER 2005

Essex's long-time scorer Clem Driver died, aged 84. He kept the scores at Chelmsford from 1979 to 1999 when he retired after a fall at Old Trafford. "Apart from the fall," he said, "the final curtain was having to put up with the dreadful music, particularly the disrespectful Hallelujah Chorus when an Essex wicket fell."

SATURDAY 26 OCTOBER 1912

Algy Gehrs scored the quickest century in Australian first class cricket when he hit a ton for South Australia against Western Australia at Adelaide. Gehrs's record stood for almost exactly seventy years – until David Hookes broke it (see 25 October 1982).

SUNDAY 26 OCTOBER 1952

Pakistan won a Test match for the first time when they beat India at University Ground, Lucknow in the second game of the 1952-1953 rubber. Of the five matches, India won two and two were drawn. For this milestone Test India won the toss and decided to bat and were dismissed for 106. Fazal Mahmood took 5 for 52. Pakistan made 331 and Nazar Mohammad carried his bat for 124 in an innings that lasted eight hours and thirty-five minutes. India were all out for 182 in their second innings and Fazal Mahmood took 7 for 42 to give him a match analysis of 12 for 94. There was certainly dancing in the streets of Lahore that night.

FRIDAY 27 OCTOBER 2000

Sri Lanka's Muttiah Muralitharan achieved the then best bowling in One Day Internationals taking 7 for 30 against India at Sharjah Cricket Association Stadium in the sixth match of the Coca-Cola Champions Trophy. Marvan Atapattu and Mahela Jayawardene both hit centuries as Sri Lanka made 294 for 5. India were then dismissed for 226 for a 68-run victory.

TUESDAY 28 OCTOBER 1986

Pakistan beat West Indies by 186 runs at Iqbal Stadium, Faisalabad in the first Test. West Indies no doubt expected to win but they were bowled out for 53, the lowest total by any team in Pakistan and the West Indians' lowest ever score, beating 76 made against Pakistan in Dacca, 1958-1959. West Indies suffered further ignominy in 1998-1999 when Australia skittled them out for 51 in Trinidad.

MUTTIAH MURALITHARAN ACHIEVED BEST ODI BOWLING FIGURES IN OCTOBER 2000

MONDAY 29 OCTOBER 1984

Mudassar Nazar scored 199 and was caught behind off Shivlal Yadav in the second Test between Pakistan and India at Iqbal Stadium, Faisalabad – the first time any batsman had been out on that figure.

SUNDAY 29 OCTOBER 2000

Sri Lanka beat India by 245 runs in the Champions Trophy final at Sharjah Cricket Association Stadium. (It remained the biggest winning margin until Australia beat Namibia by 256 runs in the 2003 World Cup.) Sri Lanka made 299 for 5 from their fifty overs with Sanath Jayasuriya hitting 189 off 161 balls with 21 fours and four sixes. India then collapsed to 54 all out with Chaminda Vaas taking 5 for 14.

SUNDAY 30 OCTOBER 1955

Imtiaz Ahmed scored 209 in 680 minutes against New Zealand to become the first wicketkeeper to score a Test double-century and also the first for Pakistan. With Waqar Hassan who scored 189 Imtiaz added a Pakistan-record 308 for the seventh wicket as his side won by four wickets.

FRIDAY 30 OCTOBER 1987

England beat Sri Lanka at Pune by eight wickets with nearly nine overs to spare to guarantee their place in the World Cup semi-final. Sri Lanka had made 218 for 7 but an opening partnership of 123 by Graham Gooch and Tim Robinson helped England to victory.

WEDNESDAY 31 OCTOBER 1917

Australian fast bowler Tibby Cotter killed by a sniper at Beersheba, Palestine when he peered over the ramparts to check what he had seen in his periscope. He had a premonition of his death and having thrown a ball of mud said to a friend, "That's my last bowl… something's going to happen."

SUNDAY 31 OCTOBER 1976

Pakistani batsman Javed Miandad became possibly the youngest player to score a double century in a Test match (at the age of 19 years, 141 days) when he hit 206 against New Zealand at National Stadium, Karachi. As with Mushtaq Mohammad's claim to be the youngest single centurion (see 12 February 1961) it is difficult to be certain of exact dates of birth for Pakistani cricketers.

CRICKET
On This Day

NOVEMBER

WEDNESDAY 1 NOVEMBER 1865

England's youngest captain Monty Bowden born at Stockwell, Surrey. He played just two Tests, both in South Africa in 1888-1889, and in the second replaced the injured C. Aubrey Smith. Bowden stayed in South Africa after the tour and died in 1892 after falling from a cart. A coffin made from whisky cases kept his corpse from being eaten by lions.

WEDNESDAY 1 NOVEMBER 1989

Pakistan won the Nehru Cup beating West Indies in the final at Eden Gardens, Calcutta by four wickets with just one ball remaining. The Windies made 273 for 5 from their overs with Desmond Haynes unbeaten on 107. Pakistan were in contention throughout with Salim Malik hitting 71 off just 62 balls. In the final over Pakistan needed three off two balls from Viv Richards who having expended his usual bowlers had to deliver the final over. Richards bowled to Wasim Akram who hit him high over midwicket for six to win the match.

SUNDAY 2 NOVEMBER 1975

Kim Hughes made his first-class debut for Western Australia against New South Wales at the Waca Ground. He scored 119 in 166 minutes and became the fifth Western Australia batsman to make a century on debut.

TUESDAY 2 NOVEMBER 1993

Pakistan leg-spinner Abdul Qadir played his last Test in a career which had seen him capture 368 wickets for his country. Pakistan beat Sri Lanka at Sharjah by two wickets. The match also marked the debut of Sri Lankan Sanath Jayasuriya.

WEDNESDAY 3 NOVEMBER 1982

On its second night Channel 4 broadcast the film *P'tang, Yang, Kipperbang*. Written by Jack Rosenthal, it tells the tale of cricket fanatic Alan Duckworth (John Albasiny) and his first kiss with Ann Lawton (Abigail Cruttenden). John Arlott voices Alan's thoughts in the style of a match commentary.

WEDNESDAY 3 NOVEMBER 2004

Playing for New South Wales against Western Australia in the Pura Cup (formerly the Sheffield Shield) at Sydney Cricket Ground, Dominic Thornely scored a maiden double century finishing on 261 not out and hitting an Australian record of eleven sixes in the process plus 21 fours. Thornely faced 367 balls in 404 minutes – beating the record score by NSW's Bobby Simpson against Western Australia and David Hookes's old record of ten sixes in an innings.

FRIDAY 4 NOVEMBER 1870

Derbyshire CCC founded at The Guildhall, Derby. The Earl of Chesterfield who had played for and against All England was the first president. Derbyshire were demoted from first class status before the 1888 season and did not regain it until 1894 and the team rejoined the County Championship in 1895. Derbyshire have only ever won the County Championship once – in 1936 and in 1920 they lost every game they played.

THURSDAY 4 NOVEMBER 1999

Fast bowler Malcolm Marshall died of colon cancer at Bridgetown, Barbados, aged 41. He had represented West Indies 81 times in Test matches and 136 times in One Day Internationals taking 376 and 157 wickets respectively. During the World Cup in 1999 it was revealed that Marshall was afflicted with cancer and he immediately resigned as coach of Hampshire and West Indies to begin treatment. It was ineffective and Marshall weighed less than four stones when he died.

SATURDAY 5 NOVEMBER 1932

Batting legend Don Bradman scored 232 for New South Wales in only 200 minutes including 32 fours.

THURSDAY 5 NOVEMBER 1964

Peter, the Lord's cat died aged 14. He lived for twelve years at the home of cricket and could often be seen prowling the outfield during big matches. The secretary of MCC said, "He was a cat of great character and loved publicity."

SATURDAY 6 NOVEMBER 1999

Australia's Michael Slater hit 169 against Pakistan at Brisbane Cricket Ground, Woolloongabba, Brisbane in the first Test. With Greg Blewett (89), he put on 269 for the first wicket (a record for Australia v Pakistan). Mark Waugh hit an even ton and Adam Gilchrist hit an 88-ball 81 in his first Test innings and Shane Warne made 86 as Australia were all out for 575. Pakistan made 281 and Australia easily made the 74-run target to win by ten wickets.

SUNDAY 6 NOVEMBER 2005

The man who represented Kerry Packer against the English cricket establishment, Bob Alexander, QC (later Baron Alexander of Weedon) died aged 69. Standing 6ft 6in, Alexander later appeared less successfully for Ian Botham after the TCCB had banned him for using cannabis. Alexander was president of MCC in 2000-2001.

THURSDAY 7 NOVEMBER 1889

The Honourable Lionel Tennyson born at Westminster, the grandson of the poet and later to become Lord Tennyson after his two elder brothers were killed in action in the Great War. Lionel Tennyson was wounded three times but survived. Tennyson played 347 matches for Hampshire between 1913 and 1935, scoring more than 12,000 runs with an average of 23.68. In the days before text messages he would send telegrams to his players. One, H.L.V. Day, received a telegram mid-innings when he was unable to cope with the Nottinghamshire fast bowlers. It read, "What do you think your blasted bat is for?" Another went to a youngster who was struggling, "For God's sake get out and let someone else take a hundred off this jam."

MONDAY 7 NOVEMBER 1955

Wallis Mathias became the first non-Muslim to play for Pakistan when he made his debut against New Zealand. The match was something of a washout with no play on three of the five days although the Kiwis were bowled out for just 70 in their first innings while Pakistan made 195 for 6 declared with Mathias scoring 41 not out. New Zealand were on 69 for 6 when the match was abandoned as a draw. Mathias played in 21 Tests over the next seven years and excelled in the slips taking 22 catches although his batting figures in Tests did not do justice to his talent. He scored 783 runs at an average of 23.72, whereas his first-class average was 44.49 from 146 matches and 7,520 runs. In 1963 he injured his finger in the nets, which left him deformed, making it difficult for him to catch the ball. He retired in 1975-1976 and died on 1 September 1994 from a brain haemorrhage, aged 59.

MONDAY 8 NOVEMBER 1976

Australian fast bowler Brett Lee born at Wollongong, New South Wales. He made his Test debut on Boxing Day 1999 against India and has played more than 70 times for his country. Not everyone is enamoured of him. Writing in *Spin*, Rob Smyth said of Lee, "He runs in like a finely tuned athlete, releases the globe like a tightly coiled spring, girls swooning at the sight of his sweeping locks – then he gets hit for twenty in an over." Another critic said, "Lee has the athleticism of an athlete, the strength of a rugby player and the backside of a National Express coach driver with a Mr Kipling habit."

SUNDAY 8 NOVEMBER 1987

Australia beat England by 7 runs in the fourth World Cup final – the first to be staged outside England. Australia won the toss and elected to bat. From their fifty overs they made 253 for 5 with David Boon top scoring on 73. England seemed to be on course for victory despite a golden duck from Tim Robinson when captain Mike Gatting was caught behind off captain Allan Border's first ball and England lost momentum and the match.

SATURDAY 9 NOVEMBER 1985

Kiwi fast bowler Richard Hadlee took nine Australian wickets for 52 at Brisbane Cricket Ground, Woolloongabba, Brisbane in the first Test of the Trans-Tasman Trophy. Hadlee also had a hand in the tenth wicket catching Geoff Lawson to give Vaughan Brown a maiden Test wicket. Hadlee finished with match figures of 15 for 123 and New Zealand won by an innings and 41 runs.

SUNDAY 9 NOVEMBER 1986

Having been bowled out for 53 in the first Test against Pakistan, West Indies took revenge in the second by winning the match by an innings and 10 runs. Malcolm Marshall took 5 for 33 as Pakistan were all out for 131, 46 of the runs coming from Javed Miandad. West Indies made 218 and opener Gordon Greenidge hit 75. A little over 200 doesn't normally guarantee an innings victory but Tony Gray and Courtney Walsh took seven wickets between them as the Windies coasted to victory.

SUNDAY 10 NOVEMBER 1991

South Africa played their first international match for 21 years – a one day international against India at Eden Gardens, Calcutta. India won the toss and elected to field. South Africa made 177 with Kepler Wessels hitting 50. India scored 178 for the loss of seven wickets with Allan Donald taking 5 for 29. Of the momentous occasion, Springbok captain Clive Rice said, "I know how Neil Armstrong felt when he stood on the moon."

FRIDAY 10 NOVEMBER 2000

Bangladesh played their first Test match. Their opponents were India at Bangabandhu National Stadium, Dhaka and they amassed 400 with Aminul Islam becoming the first Bangladeshi centurion, finally being out for 145. After India made 429 the Bangladeshis collapsed and were bowled out in their second innings for just 91, leaving India just 63 to win, a target they reached for the loss of just one wicket.

WEDNESDAY 11 NOVEMBER 1891

After scoring 271 for South Australia, George Giffen took 9 for 96 and 7 for 70 to give an innings victory over Victoria. No one else in first class cricket has taken sixteen wickets and scored a double century in a match.

TUESDAY 11 NOVEMBER 1930

Test cricketer Dodger Whysall died aged 43 of septicaemia in hospital at Nottingham. A former wicketkeeper, he made his name as a batsman but did not break through properly until after the Great War. In late October 1930 he went dancing, fell over on the dance floor and injured his elbow. The joint became infected and two weeks later he was dead.

WEDNESDAY 12 NOVEMBER 1884

Hampshire bowler Jack Newman was born at Southsea. An immensely likeable fellow, he had a number of run-ins with his captain and friend the Honourable Lionel Tennyson. During one match Newman appealed for the light and was turned down by the umpire. He made his feelings known and his batting partner Tennyson told him to behave. When it was obvious that Newman was ignoring his captain, Tennyson shouted, "Can you hear me, Newman?" to which his bowler responded, "Yes, my Lord, but where are you speaking from?" (see 31 August 1922).

SATURDAY 13 NOVEMBER 1982

On the second day of the Perth Test between Australia and England Aussie bowler Terry Alderman severely dislocated his right shoulder when he rugby tackled Gary Donnison, an "objectionable and semi-drunk" unemployed 19-year-old Englishman who had hit Alderman on the head during a pitch invasion. "I have played a bit of Aussie Rules and I know what a gentle tap is and what a thump to the head is, and that was a thump to the back of the head," Alderman recalled. "With that he ran off, and I could see that there were no police in the vicinity so I attempted to apprehend him." As the two men wrestled on the ground Donnison threw a punch at Alderman who later said, "I can't remember a lot of how I fell... but I was immediately aware I was injured... it was very painful indeed."Teammates Dennis Lillee and Allan Border hauled Donnison off Alderman and held him until the police arrived. England bowler Bob Willis was not overly sympathetic. "For a remote and sleepy city, Perth had a surprisingly large hard core of hooligans," he said. "However, Terry was stupid to head off in pursuit of that idiot and the injury set back his career a lot." It would be a year before Alderman could bowl in a competitive match. Donnison was found guilty of assault and was fined A$500 and ordered to do 200 hours of community service.

TUESDAY 13 NOVEMBER 1990

A cricketing metaphor brought down a prime minister. Having resigned as Deputy Prime Minister and Leader of the House of Commons over Margaret Thatcher's opposition to the European Union, Sir Geoffrey Howe, in a devastating resignation speech, said of his leader, "I hope that there is no monopoly of cricketing metaphors. It is rather like sending your opening batsmen to the crease only for them to find, the moment the first balls are bowled, that their bats have been broken before the game by the team captain." The following day Michael Heseltine announced he was standing for party leadership and on 22 November, two days after she had failed to see him off by just four votes, Mrs Thatcher resigned as premier after eleven and a half years in the job.

MONDAY 14 NOVEMBER 1921

South Africa opening batsman Billy Zulch was out in unusual circumstances in the second Test against Australia at Old Wanderers, Johannesburg. Having scored 4, Zulch prepared to face Ted McDonald. He hit the ball but in doing so broke his bat, a piece of which careered into the stumps leaving him out "hit wicket".

FRIDAY 14 NOVEMBER 2008

India beat England by 158 runs in the one day international at Madhavrao Scindia Cricket Ground, Rajkot. England won the toss and chose to field first which was a huge mistake. India made 387 for 5 the highest ODI total against England in history.

SATURDAY 15 NOVEMBER 1947

Australian batting legend Don Bradman scored his hundredth first class century playing for an Australian XI against the Indians touring side. Indians won the toss and decided to bat and made 326 and not one player hit three figures. The Australian XI made 380 with Bradman hitting 172 at the Sydney Cricket Ground. It was his 295th innings but the Indians did not let him celebrate as they won by 47 runs.

WEDNESDAY 15 NOVEMBER 2000

Pakistani off-break bowler Saqlain Mushtaq played in his first Test against England, and picked up 8 wickets for 164 at Gaddafi Stadium, Lahore. He thus became the first bowler to take five or more wickets on his first appearance against four Test countries.

WEDNESDAY 16 NOVEMBER 1977

A team led by Ian Chappell met one captained by Richie Robinson who was also the wicketkeeper at Moorabbin Oval, Melbourne in what was the first game of World Series Cricket – a two-day, 75-over match. I.M. Chappell's XI batted first and made 273 for 9 declared with wicketkeeper Rodney Marsh the top scorer on 59. Ray Bright took 5 for 54. R.D. Robinson's XI were bowled out for 271 meaning Chappell's side won by two runs. Admission was free.

MONDAY 16 NOVEMBER 1981

Australian fast bowler Dennis Lillee and Pakistani captain Javed Miandad involved in what *Wisden* described as "one of the most undignified incidents in Test history". It happened at Perth during the first of three Tests in Pakistan's second innings. Miandad hit Lillee for a single but as he ran he bumped into Lillee. Miandad claimed that Lillee had kicked him and in retaliation he made as if to hit the pace man with his bat – umpire Tony Crafter had to step between the two players. Former Australian captain Bobby Simpson called it "the most disgraceful thing I have seen on a cricket field" while Keith Miller demanded that Lillee be suspended for the rest of the season. The Australian team dictated punishments in those days and they fined Lillee A\$200. When the umpires complained that was too lenient the Australian Board cut the fine to A\$120 but banned Lillee for two matches.

FRIDAY 17 NOVEMBER 1876

Major Hesketh Vernon Hesketh-Prichard, DSO, MC, FRGS, FZS born at Jhansi, Uttar Pradesh, India. A renaissance man, he was an explorer, adventurer, big-game hunter and marksman and also a fine fast bowler for Hampshire and MCC. Her made his first class debut for Hampshire against Somerset during the County Championship in 1900. He toured the West Indies with Lord Brackley's XI in 1904-1905 and in 1907 went to the United States with MCC. His career best was 8 for 32 for Hampshire against Derbyshire in July 1905. Hesketh-Prichard died from sepsis on 14 June 1922.

SATURDAY 17 NOVEMBER 1900

Australian and England Test fast bowler J.J. Ferris died aged 33 of enteric fever at Addington, Durban, Natal, South Africa while serving with the Army in the Boer War. Born at Sydney, New South Wales he made his Test debut for Australia at Sydney in 1886-1887 where he bowled England out for 45. He played eight times for his country. He emigrated to England where he played for Gloucestershire. In 1891-1892 he played for England in one Test, at Cape Town, where he took 13 for 91.

SATURDAY 18 NOVEMBER 2000

Andy Flower hit an unbeaten 183 for Zimbabwe in the first Test against India in Delhi, and in the following 13 months he scored 1,466 runs with an average of 133.27, including five tons and seven fifties. He finished the year as the world's top batsman.

SATURDAY 19 NOVEMBER 1938

MCC won the toss against Griqualand West at De Beers Stadium, Kimberley and elected to bat. By the time their innings ended the next day they had scored 676 – the highest total in South African first class cricket. The majority of the runs came from Len Hutton (149), Bill Edrich (109), Eddie Paynter (158) and Norman Yardley (142). The MCC wickets were shared equally between James McNally (5 for 154) and Eric Franz (5 for 105). Master spinner Hedley Verity took 7 for 22 as Griqualand West collapsed to 114 all out. Verity took 4 for 44 as Griqualand West followed on and they were all out for 273 as MCC won by an innings and 289 runs.

FRIDAY 19 NOVEMBER 1976

India completed their first innings in the second Test against New Zealand at Green Park, Kanpur. Captain Bishan Bedi declared at 524 for 9 – the highest Test innings total which did not include a century. The top scorer was Mohinder Amarnath with 70. The two lowest scores were Brijesh Patel with 13 and Bhagwath Chandrasekhar 10 not out. Bedi scored a Test career best 50 not out that included three sixes and three fours. The match ended in a draw.

TUESDAY 20 NOVEMBER 2001

A controversial Test match ended in a draw at Crusaders Ground, St George's Park, Port Elizabeth between South Africa and India. After the game match referee Mike Denness issued sanctions against six of the Indian team. He issued punishments to Sachin Tendulkar for ball tampering (one Test match suspended ban), Virender Sehwag for excessive appealing (one Test match ban), Sourav Ganguly for the inability to control his team's behaviour (one Test match ban and two one day international matches suspended ban), Harbhajan Singh for excessive appealing (one Test match suspended ban), Shiv Sundar Das for excessive appealing (one Test match suspended ban) and Deep Dasgupta also for excessive appealing (one Test Match suspended ban). The incident caused uproar in India where the excitable natives burnt Denness's image in effigy. The Board of Control for Cricket in India threatened to call off its tour of South Africa unless Denness was replaced as match referee for the third Test. The United Cricket Board of South Africa agreed with its Indian counterpart and refused Denness entrance to the ground on the first day of the third Test. The ICC responded by stripping the planned third game of Test match status. The ICC also insisted that Virender Sehwag serve his one-match ban (due to be against England in India) but the BCCI selected him at which point the ICC announced that it would refuse to recognise any match with Sehwag in the India side. After negotiations, India dropped Sehwag from the team for the first Test against England. An ICC Disputes Resolution Committee was due to hear India's appeal on 6-7 June 2002 but it was postponed because Denness underwent heart surgery.

SATURDAY 20 NOVEMBER 2004

After 102 matches Glenn McGrath scored his maiden Test half century – the longest time anyone has taken to achieve the milestone. The achievement came in the first Test of the Trans-Tasman Trophy between

Australia and New Zealand at Brisbane Cricket Ground, Woolloongabba, Brisbane. With Jason Gillespie McGrath shared in a last wicket stand of 114 but McGrath's final tally of 61 was the highest score made by an Australian number eleven. Sri Lankan Muttiah Muralitharan is next on the list of having to wait for the maiden half-century but he achieved his in his 64th Test – almost forty sooner than McGrath.

WEDNESDAY 21 NOVEMBER 1973

The first match played in the Deodhar Trophy – the first limited overs competition in India. South and East Zones contested the game at M.A. Chidambaram Stadium, Chepauk, Madras and each side was limited to 60 overs per innings. East Zone batted first and Abid Ali bowled the initial delivery to Probir Hazarika. Abid Ali took Hazarika's wicket for 11 caught behind by Syed Kirmani. South Zone needed just 51.3 of their overs to score 157 and win the match by five wickets.

SATURDAY 22 NOVEMBER 1969

The first limited overs first class match played in Australia. The Vehicle and General Insurance Group sponsored competition saw Victoria (131 for 2) easily beat Tasmania (130 for 9) by eight wickets. Tasmania's Kevin Brown scored the first run of the competition in the first over from Alan Thomson. Baden Sharman's was the first wicket to fall, caught behind by Norman Carlyon off Robert Rowan. Ken Eastwood (69) scored the first half-century in the competition.

FRIDAY 22 NOVEMBER 1974

The first Test match was played at Bangalore between India and West Indies. It also marked the first time that Clive Lloyd had captained the Windies and the first Test appearances of Gordon Greenidge and Viv Richards and Greenidge doubly celebrated by becoming the first West Indian to score a ton on his debut. India won the toss and elected to field. The Windies made 289 (Alvin Kallicharran 124, Greenidge 93, Bhagwath Chandrasekhar 4 for 112) and in reply India hit 260 (Hemant Kanitkar 65, Syed Abid Ali 49). The tourists then made 356 for 6 declared (Lloyd 163, Greenidge 107) but Indian captain the Nawab of Pataudi Jr and wicketkeeper Farokh Engineer were both injured while fielding and unable to bat in India's second innings. West Indies bowled out India's eight men for 118 to win the match by 267 runs before lunch on the fifth day.

SUNDAY 23 NOVEMBER 1755

Thomas Lord – the man who gave his name to the home of cricket – born at Thirsk, Yorkshire. In 1787 with the encouragement and financial help of George Finch, 9th Earl of Winchilsea and Charles Lennox, 4th Duke of Richmond, Lord bought a seven-acre site at Dorset Square where he founded his first cricket ground.

THURSDAY 23 NOVEMBER 2006

British police showed once again that they are the best in the world – by confiscating a cricket ball being carried by a fan on the way to watch a match because it was a "potentially lethal weapon". Chris Hurd, a 28-year-old accountant with Ernst & Young, was on his way to watch the first Ashes Test in a pub with friends when he was stopped by a WPC at Baker Street on the London Underground. He said, "She was completely humourless and inflexible, and showed no understanding of my excitement about the Ashes. She asked if I was aware I was carrying a very hard object and I said, 'Yes, it is a cricket ball.' She told me I should not be carrying it in public because it was a potentially lethal weapon. I was wearing a boring suit and looked every inch the bean counter I am. It is not as if I was unshaven and looked dangerous. But she confiscated the ball for most of our conversation, gave me a verbal warning and said she was being very lenient. She filled out a stop-and-search form and finally gave the ball back and sent me packing."

FRIDAY 24 NOVEMBER 1989

Sachin Tendulkar, at 16 years 214 days, became the youngest player to make a Test fifty when he hit 59 in the second Test between India and Pakistan at Iqbal Stadium, Faisalabad. The match ended in stalemate.

TUESDAY 24 NOVEMBER 1998

Bad weather saved England from almost certain defeat in the first Test in Brisbane, Australia. Needing 348 to win, England were struggling on 179 for 6 when the heavens opened.

SATURDAY 25 NOVEMBER 1950

Bombay Governor's XI played the Commonwealth XI at the Brabourne Stadium, Bombay. The Governor's XI captain Raja Maharaj Singh won the toss and decided to bat. Nothing unusual in that except at the time of the match he was 72 years old, having been born on 17 May 1878 at

Kapurthala, Punjab, India, and was making his only first-class appearance. Bombay Governor's XI made 202 in their first innings with Rusi Modi making 68 and Jim Laker taking 4 for 61. Commonwealth XI made 483 for 5 declared with Emmett scoring 96, Ken Grieves 132, Dick Spooner 57, Derek Shackleton 55 and Eddie Paynter an unbeaten 75. In their second innings Bombay Governor's XI were all out for 108 with George Tribe taking 8 for 23. The effort was too much for pensioner captain Singh; he was absent from his team's second knock. The Commonwealth XI won by an innings and 173 runs.

FRIDAY 26 NOVEMBER 1948

Pakistan played its first representative match – albeit not a Test match – against West Indies at Bagh-e-Jinnah Ground, Lahore. Pakistan won the toss and elected to bat. In their first innings they made 241 with the majority of their runs coming from their openers Nazar Muhammad (87) and wicketkeeper Imtiaz Ahmed (76). West Indies scored 308 in their first innings with 55 from Everton Weekes and 72 from Kenneth Rickards. Pakistan declared their second innings at 285 for 6 with the top scores coming from Imtiaz Ahmed (131) and captain Mian M Saeed (101). When play ended West Indies were on 98 for 1 and the match finished in a draw.

MONDAY 26 NOVEMBER 1984

Kim Hughes burst into tears as he announced his resignation as captain of the Australia Test side. He had just led the Aussies to defeat in the second Test at Brisbane against West Indies and at the post-match press conference, Hughes began to read a prepared statement to the press. "The constant speculation, criticism and innuendo by former players and sections of the media have taken their toll," he said. "In the interest of the team, Australian cricket and myself, I have informed the ACB of my decision to stand down as Australian captain." Hughes began weeping, stood up, handed the statement to Bob Merriman, the Australian manager, who was sitting next to him and, head bowed, left the room. Merriman finished reading the text. Years later, he said, "When I sat there in the press conference I just couldn't stop myself. It was an emotional thing to do and I don't regret doing it. There was no media manager as well at that time; you had to fend for yourself." Although he had stepped down as skipper, he said he wanted to continue as a player and perhaps to assuage their own guilt, the selectors retained him for two more Tests. He scored nought, two, nought and nought.

FRIDAY 27 NOVEMBER 1970

The Home Guard of Walmington-on-Sea were challenged to a game of cricket by the ARP wardens – which is how former fast bowler Fiery Fred Trueman came to appear in the situation comedy *Dad's Army*. Trueman played a ringer Ernie C. Egan invited to play by Chief ARP Warden Hodges (Bill Pertwee) but he strained his arm and had to drop out. Can the Home Guard win the day?

FRIDAY 27 NOVEMBER 1987

England opener Chris Broad refused to walk after being given out in his second innings of the first Test against Pakistan at Gaddafi Stadium, Lahore. England had won the toss and decided to bat and were all out for 175. Abdul Qadir took a Test career best 9 for 56. Pakistan made 392 all out with Mudassar Nazar scoring 120. Graham Gooch and Broad then opened the second innings and when he had scored 13 he faced Iqbal Qasim. Broad played forward, missed the ball totally and was amazed when the umpire Shakeel Khan gave him out caught behind by Ashraf Ali. It was only the intervention of Gooch that finally persuaded Broad to leave the crease. To add to the misery, England were bowled out for 130 and Pakistan won by an innings and 87 runs.

WEDNESDAY 28 NOVEMBER 1979

England beat West Indies on a faster run rate in the one day international in the Benson & Hedges World Series Cup at Sydney Cricket Ground. The match was not without controversy as with West Indies needing three to win England captain Mike Brearley put all his fielders – including wicketkeeper David Bairstow – on the boundary.

THURSDAY 28 NOVEMBER 1996

The second Test between Pakistan and New Zealand at Rawalpindi Cricket Stadium began twenty minutes late because nobody thought to bring a ball and one had to be bought from a local sports shop. The Test was also interrupted four overs into the third session for a further twenty minutes when the low-lying sun reflected off objects into the batsmen's eyes. Two players – Ijaz Ahmed of Pakistan and Kiwi Chris Cairns – were fined 50 per cent of their match fee for dissent. In the end Pakistan won by an innings and 13 runs.

PAKISTAN'S IJAZ AHMED WAS FINED HALF HIS MATCH FEE FOR DISSENT IN NOVEMBER 1996

SATURDAY 29 NOVEMBER 1952

Play finally began in the Sheffield Shield match between South Australia and New South Wales at Adelaide Oval after no play on the first day. Eccentric batsman Sid Barnes had offered to be 12th man so that Ray Flockton could get some experience (he was out for nought in the first innings as it turned out). When the players broke for drinks, Barnes came on carrying drinks in a suit and tie rather than whites. He also brought with him a radio, cigars, iced towels, a mirror and comb, and a clothes brush. The crowd's humour turned to anger when the incident delayed the match and the South Australia team officially complained to the New South Wales Cricket Association. Barnes only played once more for New South Wales. He wrote a book about the 1953 Ashes tour, which lost him friends, and eventually he killed himself. Also playing for New South Wales was Jim Burke, another cricketer who was to die by his own hand.

SUNDAY 29 NOVEMBER 1970

On the third day of the first Test against Australia Colin Cowdrey beat Wally Hammond's record of most runs scored in Test cricket (7,249) when he scored 22 at Woolloongabba, Brisbane. He only added six more before Ian Chappell caught him off John Gleeson's bowling.

FRIDAY 30 NOVEMBER 1962

The Reverend David Sheppard became the first ordained minister to play Test cricket. He had made his debut in 1950, five years before he was ordained into the Anglican Church. In 1954 he was captain for two Tests against Pakistan but his clerical duties took up much of his time and he disappeared from the Test scene. He was recalled in 1962 against Pakistan and did well enough to be included on the Ashes winter tour. Opening the batting for England Sheppard scored 31 and 53. His Test career ended in 1963 and he went on to become Bishop of Woolwich and Bishop of Liverpool before his death from bowel cancer on 5 March 2005.

TUESDAY 30 NOVEMBER 1999

Zimbabwe beat Pakistan by seven wickets at Peshawar to record their first overseas Test win.

CRICKET
On This Day

DECEMBER

SUNDAY 1 DECEMBER 1940

England Test captain Mike Denness born at Bellshill, North Lanarkshire, Scotland. He appeared in 28 Tests for England but left after the first Test of the 1975 rubber against Australia. The Aussies had been England's opponents in the previous series and Denness had dropped himself because of his poor form. One Australian sent him a letter with the address "Mike Denness, cricketer" on the envelope. Denness opened it and inside was a note reading, "Should this reach you, the post office clearly thinks more of your ability than I do."

FRIDAY 2 DECEMBER 1977

With twelve of the tourists to England the previous summer defecting to Kerry Packer's World Series Cricket, Australia were short of players for the opening Test against India in the 1977-78 series. Bobby Simpson was recalled for his first Test since 1967-68 and Australia fielded six debutants – only Simpson, Gary Cosier, Craig Serjeant, Jeff Thomson and Alan Hurst having previous Test experience. Thomson had signed for Packer but changed his mind. Australia won the toss and elected to bat scoring 166 (debutant Peter Toohey 82, Bishan Bedi 5 for 55) and 327 (Simpson 89, Toohey 57, Madan Lal 5 for 72) against India's 153 (Dilip Vengsarkar 48, Gundappa Viswanath 45, Wayne Clark 4 for 46) and 324 (Sunil Gavaskar 113, Thomson 4 for 76, Clark 4 for 101) and winning the match by 16 runs – the then eighth narrowest victory in Test cricket.

FRIDAY 2 DECEMBER 1977

Meanwhile at the VFL Park, Melbourne the first "Supertest" began between WSC Australia and WSC West Indies. The tourists won the toss and elected to field. WSC Australia made 256 in their first innings with the top score coming from spin bowler Ray Bright with 69. Opener Rick McCosker, Greg Chappell and great white hope David Hookes all went for a duck. Michael Holding took 4 for 60. WSC West Indies hit 214 with Viv Richards hitting 79 and the WSC Windies' wickets being spread between Dennis Lillee, Len Pascoe, Max Walker, Hookes and Bright. WSC Australia made 192 in their second knock with 110 of the runs coming from McCosker (47) and Hookes (63). Andy Roberts was the most successful WSC Windies bowler with 4 for 52. The target to reach was 235 and WSC West Indies won by three wickets when they achieved 237 for 7.

WEDNESDAY 3 DECEMBER 1890

Billy Midwinter, the first player to play for and against Australia in Test matches died aged 39 at Kew Insane Asylum, Princess Street and Yarra Boulevard, Kew, Melbourne, Victoria, Australia. Born at Lower Meend, St Briavels, Gloucestershire on 19 June 1851, he emigrated Down Under with his family in 1860. He made his Test debut for Australia in the inaugural match in 1877, scoring 5 and 17 and taking 5 for 78 off 54 overs in the first innings and 1 for 23 off 19 overs in the second. Returning to England, he played for Gloucestershire where he stayed until 1882. He was selected to play for England against the Old Enemy on the 1881-1882 tour and scored 40 in the first Test which began on 31 December 1881. He played in all four Tests against Australia on that tour but a year later was back in Australia's green cap playing against England. In all he played in a dozen Tests, eight for Australia against England and four for England against Australia. He went mad with grief after the death of his wife and two children.

SUNDAY 3 DECEMBER 1961

It's only a game – at the end of a controversial match between High Bridge Hotel and Mount Erica Hotel at Albert Park, Melbourne High Bridge captain W.J. Young remonstrated with umpire E.J. Mangan. What started off as verbal quickly became physical and the umpire ended up spending a month in hospital while Young was sentenced to two months in prison.

MONDAY 4 DECEMBER 1950

Australia declared their second innings on the third day of the first Test against England at Woolloongabba, Brisbane, Queensland having scored a meagre 32 for 7. The rain had given the wicket its usual sticky feel at the Gabba and having won the toss and elected to bat Australia made 228 all out with Neil Harvey top scoring on 74. Alec Bedser was the most successful England bowler taking 4 for 45 with Trevor Bailey a close second on 3 for 28. England made just 68 for 7 before declaring with just three players achieving double figures. Australian captain Lindsay Hassett declared on 32 for 7, leaving England a target of 193 to win. Sadly, they were unable to rise to the occasion and the Aussies bowled them out for 122, winning by 70 runs.

SATURDAY 5 DECEMBER 1959

Indian cricketing legend Duleep died at Bombay aged 54. Kumar Shri Duleepsinhji Jadeja, to give him his full name, played for Cambridge University, Sussex and England before his career was cut short by illness. In a dozen Tests he averaged 58.52 from 995 runs with a top score of 173. The Duleep Trophy is named in his honour. His uncle was Kumar Shri Ranjitsinhji Vibhaji Jadeja, Maharaja Jam Sahib of Nawanagar.

TUESDAY 5 DECEMBER 2000

Former Indian captain Mohammad Azharuddin banned from playing cricket for life after being found guilty of match fixing. Azharuddin and fellow Test player Ajay Sharma both received life bans from the Board of Control for Cricket in India. Azharuddin confessed to fixing three One Day Internationals. Sharma, a promising player, managed just one Test appearance before his ban for associating with bookies. The BCCI lifted the ban on Azharuddin in 2006 (see 6 March 2000).

TUESDAY 6 DECEMBER 1977

Lancashire and England all-rounder Andrew "Freddie" Flintoff born in Preston. Standing 6ft 4in, Freddie – the nickname comes because of the closeness of his surname to Flintstone – made his Test debut when he was 20 but success came too quickly and thanks to a copious appetite for drink and fast food, he weighed in at 18 stone. Knuckling down, Flintoff in 2005 was recognised as England's best all-rounder since Ian Botham. In the Ashes series that year he scored 402 runs and took two dozen wickets which led to his winning the BBC Sports Personality of the Year, ICC Player of the Year and the PCA Player of the Year (for the second year running) as well as being awarded the MBE.

MONDAY 7 DECEMBER 1992

The first official one day international in South Africa saw the home side beat India at Newlands, Cape Town. India made 184 with Hansie Cronje taking 5 for 32. The future corrupt captain was also at the crease (12 not out) as South Africa won by 6 wickets with three balls remaining. Captain Kepler Wessels was the first man to be given out by the video-watching umpire in an ODI.

TUESDAY 8 DECEMBER 1987

England captain Mike Gatting had a stand-up row with square leg umpire Shakoor Rana during the last over of the second day of the second Test at Faisalabad. With Pakistan at 106 for 5, Eddie Hemmings bowled his fourth ball of the over and umpire Khizar Hayat called "Dead ball" because Gatting had supposedly moved a fielder (David Capel) without the batsman's knowledge. Rana stopped the game and claimed that Gatting was guilty of unfair play under Law 42. Gatting and the umpire had a heated row. Gatting was later heard saying, "One rule for one, one for another", after his appeal for a catch was turned down. Rana demanded an apology saying, "[Gatting] just abused me. I cannot tell you what did he say but he used filthy language, bad language" (believed to be the words "You f***ing, cheating c***" although some sources report that the words were said by Rana to Gatting). The row meant that there was no play on the third day and eventually the TCCB and Foreign Office became involved. The TCCB forced Gatting to apologise (Rana kept the note under his pillow) and the game continued although it ended in a draw. Rana said later, "I do not regret what happened. How can I regret? It made me the most famous umpire. People don't recognise me now. But when I introduce myself everyone says, 'Ah, yes, the famous umpire'." He met Gatting again in England a few years later. "I wanted to shake his hand," recalled the umpire, "but he said, 'Oh God, not you again,' and drove away."

MONDAY 8 DECEMBER 2008

Former England cricketer Chris Lewis arrested at Gatwick Airport on suspicion of smuggling into Britain nine pounds of cocaine, worth about £140,000. The drugs were found in baggage removed from a flight from Saint Lucia. On 20 May 2009 he was sentenced at Croydon Crown Court to thirteen years in prison and claimed that his friend Chad Kirnon, a former basketball player for London Towers, had set him up. Judge Nicholas Ainley said, "In a cowardly attempt to evade justice, you each sought to blame the other for a crime you obviously jointly committed. Drug smugglers would not entrust a valuable cargo like this to an innocent traveller. You were knowingly and willingly engaged in major organised crime." Former teammate Angus Fraser said, "As a person, Chris liked the nice things in life, the clothes and the cars, but once his playing days were over, his means of income was reduced. He needed the money and it appears he got dragged into something like this. It's very sad."

WEDNESDAY 9 DECEMBER 1992

India all-rounder Kapil Dev ran out South Africa's Peter Kirsten while he was backing up too far in a one day international at Crusaders Ground, St George's Park, Port Elizabeth. When the umpire gave Kirsten out, he refused to leave the pitch until the officials insisted. Kirsten was later fined 50 per cent of his match fee for dissent. The good news was that South Africa won by 6 wickets with 20 balls remaining.

SATURDAY 9 DECEMBER 1995

On the second morning of the first Test between Australia and Sri Lanka at Western Australia Cricket Association Ground, Perth umpires Khizer Hayat and Peter Parker decided that a Sri Lankan had been doctoring the seam of the ball. The tourists vehemently denied the allegation but became the first side to be found guilty of ball tampering although the decision was reversed a fortnight later. Australia won the match by an innings and 36 runs. The game also marked the sole Test of Stuart Law, the Queensland, Essex, Derbyshire and Lancashire batsman who became a British citizen in 2004.

WEDNESDAY 10 DECEMBER 1958

Australia (186 and 147 for 2) beat England (134 and 198) by eight wickets in the first Test match televised in Australia. The first Test held at Brisbane Cricket Ground, Woolloongabba, Brisbane was also notable for England's Trevor Bailey taking seven hours and 38 minutes to score 68 in the second innings. Peter May set a Test record by captaining England for the 26th time.

FRIDAY 11 DECEMBER 1992

Batsman Dirk Wellham became the first player to captain three Australian states when he led out Queensland, having previously been in charge at New South Wales and Tasmania.

SUNDAY 11 DECEMBER 2005

Andrew "Freddie" Flintoff became the first cricketer for 24 years to win the BBC Sports Personality of the Year Award. He saw off the challenge of sailor Ellen MacArthur, with Liverpool footballer Steven Gerrard in third place. Flintoff was presented with the trophy in Pakistan where he was on tour with England. The presenter was Ian Botham, the last cricketing winner in 1981.

FRIDAY 12 DECEMBER 1884

The Adelaide Oval became the second Test ground with the word "oval" in its name. The spire of St Peter's Cathedral looms over the ground, which opened in 1873 amid furious local arguments over boundaries and money. The first Test (a timeless one) was beset by problems over appearance money and three umpires took turns in standing. It was at the Adelaide Oval in 1932-1933 that police had to patrol the boundaries to keep the 50,962 crowd in check after Bill Woodfull and Bert Oldfield were struck by England bowlers.

FRIDAY 12 DECEMBER 1930

The first Australia-West Indies Test match began. A timeless match held at the Adelaide Oval, West Indies won the toss and decided to bat. They made 296 all out with Clarrie Grimmett taking 7 for 87. Australia replied with 376, Alan Kippax hitting a Test career best 146. The West Indians made 249 in their second innings but Bill Ponsford and Archie Jackson took the Aussies to a ten-wicket victory with 172 for 0 off 55.3 overs.

FRIDAY 13 DECEMBER 1901

Archie MacLaren scored the first Test century-plus of the twentieth century when he hit 116 against Australia at Sydney Cricket Ground.

TUESDAY 13 DECEMBER 1988

Having won the toss and decided to bat, West Indies (220: Desmond Haynes 78, Gordon Greenidge 52) beat Australia (219 for 8: David Boon 71) by one run in the Benson & Hedges World Series Cup One Day International.

WEDNESDAY 14 DECEMBER 1960

The first tie in Test cricket occurred between Australia led by Richie Benaud and West Indies under the captaincy of Frank Worrell at the Brisbane Cricket Ground, Woolloongabba, Brisbane. The West Indies won the toss and elected to bat making 453 with Gary Sobers hitting 132. Australia made 505 with Norm O'Neill hitting a Test best of 181 and Wes Hall taking 4 for 140. In their second innings the Windies hit 284 leaving Australia 233 to win in 310 minutes. At one stage they were 232 for 8 before wicketkeeper Wally Grout was run out on 2. Last man Lindsay Kline came in with just one run needed but as he and Ian Meckiff went for it, Meckiff, too, was run out for 2 on the seventh ball of the final over leaving the scores tied.

SUNDAY 15 DECEMBER 2002

Australia beat England by 89 runs at Melbourne Cricket Ground in the 2002-2003 VB Series. Australia won the toss and decided to bat and made 318 for 6 from their fifty overs. Wicketkeeper and opening batsman Adam Gilchrist scored 124 and captain Ricky Ponting 119. England were all out for 229. Fast medium pace bowler James Anderson made his debut in the match because of an injury to Andy Caddick with the result he took to the field in a shirt without his name or squad number. One Australian fan was not amused. "Hey, Pom," he shouted, "are you too f***ing embarrassed to have your name on your shirt?"

MONDAY 15 DECEMBER 2008

Don Bradman's 1948 England tour cap sold for a loss after being passed in at auction in Melbourne. The hat eventually sold for around A$400,000 (£175,375), several thousand dollars less than the seller had paid for it in 2003. Auctioneer Charles Leski refused to reveal the exact price but said it was more than A$400,000 and below the A$420,000 that seller Tim Serisier paid for it in England helped by his winnings from the television programme *Who Wants To Be A Millionaire?* The cap failed to attract a single bid at auction, despite predictions it could fetch more than A$750,000.

SATURDAY 16 DECEMBER 1916

South Africa Test wicket keeper Tom Campbell, aged 34, fell out of the Cape mail train from Johannesburg. He was found by another train driver unconscious by the side of the track and taken to Krugersdorp Hospital where it was discovered that he had concussion and other head injuries. His life hung in the balance for some time but eventually he recovered. Ironically, eight years later, on the morning of 5 October 1924, he was killed in a mail train crash at Milndale near Durban.

SATURDAY 16 DECEMBER 1978

West Indies fast bowler Malcolm Marshall, 20, on his Test debut against India at Bangalore was given out lbw to Bhagwat Chandrasekhar but claimed that he had hit the ball. Umpire Mohammad Ghouse was unmoved and Marshall burst into tears as he made his way to the pavilion. On 17 December he took his first Test wicket C.P.S. Chauhan caught by Derrick Parry for 15. With West Indies leading by 266 runs, the match was abandoned following rioting in Bangalore after the arrest of former prime minister Indira Gandhi.

FRIDAY 17 DECEMBER 1920

Australian batsman and bookie Herbie "Horseshoe" Collins made his Test debut against England at Sydney Cricket Ground and on opening the batting was run out for 70. In his first four knocks he scored 70, 104, 64 and 162 to make him statistically the most successful "beginner" in Test cricket.

SATURDAY 17 DECEMBER 2005

Darren Gough won the third series of the BBC's terpsichorean talent show *Strictly Come Dancing*. With partner Lilia Kopylova, Gough beat TV presenters Bill Turnbull, Fiona Phillips, Gloria Hunniford and Zoë Ball, former snooker player Dennis Taylor, actresses Patsy Palmer, Jaye Jacobs and Siobhan Hayes, actor Will Thorp, chef James Martin and sprinter Colin Jackson. Gough was originally an unwilling participant. He moaned, "I can't dance like a nancy on national TV."

TUESDAY 18 DECEMBER 1979

Australian fast bowler Dennis Lillee threw a strop and an aluminium bat "fully 40 yards towards the pavilion" after England captain Mike Brearley complained about its use on the fourth day of the first Test at the WACA Cricket Ground in Perth. Lillee employed the bat as a publicity stunt for a friend's company and had used it previously against West Indies without incident. However, after hitting a three Brearley told the umpires that he believed the ball had been damaged. Captain Greg Chappell sent out 12th man Rodney Hogg with a traditional willow bat but Lillee refused to change until Chappell himself came out and insisted. Lillee eventually scored 19 before Peter Willey caught him off Graham Dilley and Australia won the Test, which was not an Ashes match by 138 runs. In 1980 the laws of the game were changed to outlaw bats not made of wood.

SUNDAY 19 DECEMBER 1976

Essex left-arm seamer John Lever took 7 for 46 on his Test debut against India at Feroz Shah Kotla, Delhi. He hit 53 and then took 3 for 24 in the second innings as England won by an innings and 25 runs.

WEDNESDAY 19 DECEMBER 1979

Geoff Boycott carried his bat in the first Test in Perth and was also the first player to be left on 99 not out in a Test match. Australia beat England by 138 runs.

WEDNESDAY 20 DECEMBER 1876

James Lillywhite's XI – in reality the first England Test side – played 22 of Goulburn at Goulburn Sportsground, New South Wales as part of their tour of New Zealand and Australia. The game was interrupted for several minutes as hares and two young kangaroos invaded the pitch and refused to leave.

THURSDAY 20 DECEMBER 1894

England beat Australia in the first Test of the 1894-1895 rubber and became the first side to win a Test after being asked to follow on. It was also the first time that a Test had run to six days. Australia captained by their wicketkeeper Jack Blackham won the toss and went into bat first. They amassed a total of 586 with Syd Gregory scoring a career best 201 over 244 minutes (it was also the first double century in a Test in Australia) and George Giffen 161. For England Tom Richardson took 5 wickets at a cost of 181. England made a more than respectable 325 with all but three players reaching double figures but none achieving a ton. Blackham enforced the follow-on and England made 437 with A Ward (who had also top scored in the first innings with 75) hitting 117. Giffen showed his prowess with the ball by taking 4 for 75 and 4 for 164 in England's innings. Australia went into bat and England bowled them out for 166 to win the match by 10 runs. Bobby Peel took 6 wickets for 67.

TUESDAY 21 DECEMBER 1920

There is no mention of the cause of death of 30-year-old Dr Claude Tozer in his *Wisden* obituary confining itself to singing his praises. In fact, his mentally deranged mistress murdered him. Before the First World War his studies at medical school precluded his playing too much first-class cricket and during the Great War he enlisted in the Royal Australian Medical Corps and won the DSO. On demob, he became a GP. He began to show promise and was selected for an Australian XI against MCC in December 1920 and opened the batting, making a half-century in both innings. It was looking increasingly likely that Tozer would be selected for the Australian national side for the Ashes tour to England in 1921. He was appointed captain for New South Wales in a non-Sheffield Shield match against Queensland scheduled for 1 January 1921. It was a game he was never to play. He spent his final Christmas relaxing, visiting friends and checking up on patients. One of the latter was Dorothy Mort a married woman with two young children that he had been treating for depression and suicidal tendencies. She was rather severe looking with a prominent nose. Ten minutes after he arrived at her home four days before Christmas he was shot in the chest, temple and back of the head. His murderer then took an overdose of laudanum and shot herself in the breast. Mort recovered and went on trial in March 1921 and it was revealed that although there was inappropriate conduct they had yet to consummate their passion. In fact, Tozer had gone to see Mort that day to break off the affair. She had already told a friend that if he did that, she would kill herself. Mort was found not guilty on the grounds of insanity, and was committed for life to an asylum, where she died twenty years later.

MONDAY 21 DECEMBER 1959

Natal beat Border by 350 runs in the Currie Cup at Jan Smuts Ground, East London. Border won the toss and decided to field on a rain-soaked pitch. Natal made 90 in 26.3 overs but would have been out for considerably less had Border not dropped five clear chances. Fast bowler Sidney Knott took 5 for 40 and medium fast bowler Athol Hagemann 5 for 49. Border went into bat and were skittled out for 16, Trevor Goddard taking six wickets for just three runs. By stumps on the first day Natal were 39 for 3 – in four hours of cricket the crowd had seen 23 wickets fall for 145 runs. Natal rallied thanks to Kim Elgie who hit a career best 162 not out as they made 294 for 8 declared. It was never going to be much of a contest – Border were dismissed for 18. Geoff Griffin – the only South African bowler to capture a Test hat-trick – who had bowled just one maiden over in the first innings took a career best 7 for 11 and wicketkeeper Malcolm Smith took seven catches as Natal won by 350 runs.

FRIDAY 22 DECEMBER 1989

The only Nobel Prize winner mentioned in *Wisden*, playwright Samuel Beckett died in Paris, France aged 83. In 1925 and 1926 he played two first-class games for Dublin University against Northamptonshire. He hit 35 runs in his four innings as a left-hand opening batsman and conceded 64 runs without taking a wicket. He won the Nobel Prize for Literature in 1969.

SUNDAY 22 DECEMBER 1996

Zimbabwe (376: Andy Flower 112 and 234) drew with England (406: Nick Knight 56, Nasser Hussain 113, John Crawley 112, Paul Strang 5 for 123 and 204 for 6: Knight 96, Alec Stewart 73) at Queens Sports Club, Bulawayo in the first Test match to be drawn with the scores level.

WEDNESDAY 23 DECEMBER 1835

Botanist Charles Darwin noted in his diary that he had seen young Maoris playing cricket at Waiwata on a farm run by British missionaries – the first record of the sport being played in New Zealand.

SATURDAY 23 DECEMBER 2006

Mark Ramprakash won the fourth series of the BBC television programme *Strictly Come Dancing* two weeks after he admitted a six-year affair with 27-year-old single mum Sadia Saleem. Partnering professional dancer Karen Hardy, Ramps beat off the challenge of newsreader Nicholas Owen, comedians Jimmy Tarbuck and Jan Ravens, singers Mica Paris and Emma Bunton, DJ Spoony, actresses Georgina Bouzova, Louisa Lytton and Claire King, ex-footballer Peter Schmeichel, TV presenter Carol Smillie, actor Ray Fearon and retired English rugby union player Matt Dawson. It was the second year in a row that a cricketer had won the competition, Darren Gough triumphing the year before.

SATURDAY 24 DECEMBER 1927

England played South Africa at Old Wanderers, Johannesburg in the first match of the 1927-1928 rubber. A dozen players made their Test debut in the match but perhaps the most unusual was Rony Stanyforth who was not only captain on his first game (as had Lord Harris in 1879) but had also never played first class cricket at county level before the tour. He was also the team wicketkeeper. It didn't harm – England won by 10 wickets.

SATURDAY 24 DECEMBER 1938

On the first day of the first Test of the 1938-1939 rubber between South Africa and England Wally Hammond, the England captain, became the first player to score 6,000 runs in Test cricket. He made just 24 but it was enough to send him past the milestone as England reached 422 all out. The Springboks replied with 390 before England declared on 291 for 4. When play finished on 28 December the match was drawn.

FRIDAY 25 DECEMBER 1942

Cricket came to the Far East and puzzled the Japanese who believe it had some religious significance. Commentator E.W. Swanton recalled "[The] first of the camps on the Thai-Burma railway on which we played cricket was Wampo, Christmas Day, 1942… This particular game was notable …

for what is probably the fastest hundred of all time. It was scored in about five overs by a very promising young Eurasian cricketer called Thoy, who, with graceful ease, kept hitting the ball over the huts."

THURSDAY 25 DECEMBER 1997

The one day international between India and Sri Lanka was abandoned after just 18 balls because of a dangerous pitch at Nehru Stadium, Indore.

TUESDAY 26 DECEMBER 1995

Controversial Sri Lankan spinner Muttiah Muralitharan was called for throwing by umpire Darrell Hair during the second Test between Australia and Sri Lanka at the Melbourne Cricket Ground. Hair no-balled Muralitharan seven times in three overs claiming his action was illegal. Sri Lankan captain Arjuna Ranatunga left the field of play to seek advice and on his return continued to bowl Muralitharan. The ICC cleared Muralitharan's action after biomechanical analysis at the University of Western Australia and at the University of Hong Kong in 1996. They concluded that he had a weird action, which created the "optical illusion of throwing".

MONDAY 26 DECEMBER 2005

The man who split cricket asunder died aged 68. In 1977 in a row over television rights Kerry Packer engineered a split with the Australian Cricket Board by creating World Series Cricket. With the help of England captain Tony Greig he recruited around fifty of the world's top players to play exclusively for his Channel 9. In two years of life, World Series Cricket introduced coloured clothing and night matches and under his regime players for the first time earned good money. Packer, who had a kidney transplant in 2000, had a history of serious illnesses and suffered severe health problems in the last two years of his life. *Forbes* valued his wealth at $5billion.

THURSDAY 27 DECEMBER 1894

The New Zealand Cricket Council founded in Christchurch, 34 years after the first inter-provincial match was played between Wellington and Auckland.

WEDNESDAY 28 DECEMBER 1842

The first recorded match in New Zealand saw the Blues defeat the Reds by 126 runs to 124. Afterwards the teams sat down for a feast of roast beef and plum pudding.

THURSDAY 29 DECEMBER 1960

Thirsty Australian batsman and Village People lookalike David Boon born at Launceston, Tasmania. He played in more than one hundred Tests for Australia scoring 7,422 runs but he is just as well known for his drinking abilities. On the flight to England for the 1989 Ashes series he drank 58 cans of beer on the plane. Former Aussie captain Ian Chappell was not impressed. "In my day," he reminisced, "58 beers between London and Sydney would have virtually classified you as a teetotaller."

TUESDAY 30 DECEMBER 2005

Springbok batting legend Eddie Barlow died aged 65, from a brain haemorrhage at the General Hospital, St Helier, Jersey. He made his Test debut against New Zealand at Durban on 8 December 1961. He played the last of his 30 Tests against Australia at Port Elizabeth on 5 March 1970 before South Africa were consigned to the sporting wilderness. Barlow scored more than 18,000 first class runs and in 1999 became coach to Bangladesh but was forced to leave the job the following year when he suffered a stroke.

TUESDAY 31 DECEMBER 1895

England became the first Test side in which every player's score reached double figures. Having made just 75 in the first innings, England got their act together by bowling out Australia at the Melbourne Cricket Ground for 123 with Tom Richardson taking 5 for 57. England then made 475 with captain Andrew Stoddart hitting 173 in 320 minutes and the rest of the team scores ranging from 11 to 53 – captain George Giffen took 6 for 155. Australia made 333 but it was not enough to prevent an England victory by 94 runs.

WEDNESDAY 31 DECEMBER 2005

All twelve members of the Ashes winning England team plus officials awarded gongs in the New Year's Honours List. Seen as a publicity stunt by Tony Blair and his Labour government, the awards did not meet with universal approval. Geoff Boycott said, "I feel so bad about mine I'm going to tie it round my cat. It's a joke." Liverpool FC complained that their Champions League victors Steven Gerrard and Jamie Carragher were ignored while Paul Collingwood received an MBE despite playing in just one Test and scoring just 17 runs and taking no wickets.